Content

Bonus content

A quick note before we begin: If you purchased a printed version of this book, you might also want to obtain an electronic version. The e-book can be convenient because it includes colored pictures that you can zoom in on for more details. Additionally, you can download it to your phone or computer and access it whenever you need it. You can download this book (for free) along with some extra video materials here: www.vwap.com

About me

Hi, I'm Dale, and I've been a full-time trader since 2008. I've always been very passionate about economics, finance, and trading. I went to university for finance, and I got certified as a portfolio manager and investment manager. I also obtained certification in financial derivatives. I'm proud to say that I have received proper education and certification, unlike the majority of other trading 'gurus.'

After college, I worked as a market analyst for a big brokerage, but I didn't stay long because I wanted to focus on my dream of being a full-time trader. From then on, I spent 12-15 hours every day testing different trading strategies, trying various approaches, and analyzing patterns. I traded all sorts of things like stocks, investment certificates, and automated trading systems. Right now, my main focus is manual forex trading.

When I first started trading forex, I thought I needed to find a secret Holy Grail strategy that would make me a lot of money fast. I searched for this among different trading indicators. I tried most of the common indicators with various settings, but none of them really worked in the long run.

My first real success came when I ditched all the indicators and started fresh with simple Price Action. It was the first time I felt like I was making progress. The breakthrough moment was when I combined Price Action with Volume Profile. That's when I started to see consistent results.

Later on, I looked for ways to improve my trading even more, especially in terms of timing my trades, confirming them, and finding strong combos of trade setups. That's when I added Order Flow and VWAP to my trading toolbox. I chose these because they both are volume-based indicators, which let me follow the big trading institutions that move the markets, rather than going against them.

In 2016, I started a website called www.trader-dale.com, where I teach people how to trade like I do through in-depth courses.

My courses cover Volume Profile trading, Order Flow trading, VWAP trading, and long-term investing. I provide custom-made indicators to my course members, including Volume Profile, Order Flow, VWAP, Trade Manager, Stock fundamentals indicator, Portfolio Tracker, and more.

Besides my website, I've written a couple of books that quickly became bestsellers on Amazon. The books are:

- VOLUME PROFILE: The Insider's Guide to Trading
- ORDER FLOW: Trading Setups
- Stock Investing with Volume Profile

You can also find me on other websites like www.volumeprofile.com, www.orderflow.com, and www.vwap.com, in addition to my main page, www.trader-dale.com.

What you will learn

I like things simple and right to the point, and this book will give you just that. The goal of this book is to provide you with immediately actionable information about VWAP trading without any redundant fillers.

In this book you can expect to:

- Gain an introduction to VWAP and how it's calculated.

- Understand why VWAP is a valuable tool for institutional traders.

- Learn where to get VWAP indicator.

- Explore my best battle-tested VWAP and Anchored VWAP trading strategies.

- Discover trade entry confirmation techniques.

- Explore order flow confirmation methods.

- Learn about Take Profit and stop loss placement.

- Understand how to manage risk and position sizing effectively.

- See real-world examples and case studies throughout the book.

- By the end of this book, you will have a comprehensive understanding of VWAP trading and you will be able to immediately start implementing that into your trading. Let's dive in!

Introduction to VWAP

VWAP, which stands for Value Weighted Average Price, is essentially an average price that takes into account the trading volume. It provides insight into where the average trader placed their orders.

If you find that the current price is above the VWAP and you've recently made a purchase, it means you bought at a price higher than what the average trader did. VWAP serves as a valuable reference point for traders.

What sets VWAP apart from other standard indicators like SMA (Simple Moving Average) or EMA (Exponential Moving Average) is the way it calculates. While SMA, EMA, and similar indicators rely solely on time and price data, VWAP incorporates trading volume into its calculation. This additional dimension of volume information makes VWAP a standout tool in technical analysis.

Here is the formula:

$$\frac{\text{Sum of } (Price * \text{Volume for each Trade})}{\text{Total Volume}}$$

Is this too theoretical? Let me give you an example to make the difference clear.

Example #1:

Imagine there were 1.000 shares traded at $10, and 5.000 shares traded at $20.

SMA = ($10 + $20)/2 = **$15**

VWAP = (($10 x 1.000) + ($20 x 5.000)) / 6.000 = **$18.33**

I can make the example even more extreme to show you how much SMA and VWAP can differ, and how misleading SMA could be.

Example #2:

Imagine there were only 100 shares traded at $5, and 5.000 shares traded at $20.

SMA = ($5+$20)/2 = **$12.5**

VWAP = (($5 x 100) + ($20 x 5.000)) / 5.100 = **$19.7**

Now, let's consider which indicator better reflects the market reality – SMA or VWAP. The answer is clear: VWAP! Why? Because VWAP represents the REAL average of all market participants, making it significantly distinct and more valuable than SMA, EMA, and other similar indicators.

Why does VWAP work?

Here are some significant facts to consider:

Fact #1: The majority of trading orders in the financial markets come from large trading institutions.

Fact #2: These trading institutions primarily use automated systems or algorithms to execute their trades.

Fact #3 (the key point): What's noteworthy is that many of these automated systems rely on VWAP as part of their trading strategies. Each institution may have its own unique approach, techniques, and goals when using VWAP, but the widespread use of VWAP-based systems in global trading is a critical factor to acknowledge.

By the way, to support these facts, you can refer to statements made by Kenneth Griffin, CEO of Citadel, one of the largest trading institutions, during his testimony before the Committee on Financial Services in the United States. This proves the significance of VWAP in the world of finance.

- "Today, virtually all trades executed by institutional investors are in the form of program trades such as volume-weighted average price (VWAP) and other algorithmic trades."
- "These VWAP trades are not large trades that you can—it's not like there's 10 million shares to be bought. It is a trade that is sliced into small slices, 100 or 200 shares, and executed over the course of a day, a week, or a month."
- "We use VWAP orders to execute on behalf of our hedge fund and have generated exceptional returns for pension plans and for endowments."

Here is the official source: https://www.govinfo.gov/content/pkg/CHRG-117hhrg43966/pdf/CHRG-117hhrg43966.pdf

Where to get VWAP

Unfortunately, neither VWAP nor Anchored VWAP is a standard indicator typically included in every trading platform. You can either search the internet for free versions of these indicators, although they often vary in quality, or you can purchase them from various vendors.

The most cost-effective option is to use the TradingView charting platform. However, the free version does not include these indicators, so you will need to purchase a subscription. The most affordable option, called "Essentials," should suffice. You can subscribe here: www.tradingview.com

Another option is to purchase my **VWAP Pack**, which includes a 9-hour VWAP video course as well as my custom-made indicators for NinjaTrader 8, TradingView, and Metatrader 4 & 5. The advantage of this package is that my indicators are compatible with the free versions of NinjaTrader and TradingView, so there are no additional costs beyond the initial purchase. This purchase includes a lifetime license and can be used on multiple computers.

You can get the **VWAP Pack** here:

https://www.trader-dale.com/vwap-training-course-and-indicators/

VWAP Trading strategies

In the next chapter, I'll explain my VWAP trading strategies. You can use these strategies for any type of trading, with any kind of trading instrument and timeframe.

My favorite trading instruments for intraday trading are major forex pairs like EUR/USD, AUD/USD, GBP/USD, and also indexes like the S&P 500. When it comes to longer-term or swing trading, I also include stocks.

For intraday trading, I prefer using 5 or 30-minute timeframes, and for swing trading, I prefer the Daily timeframe.

You don't have to learn all of these strategies at once; it might be too overwhelming. I suggest choosing a couple that you like and feel comfortable with, and starting with those.

Strategy #1 – Reactions to VWAP

Strategy description

The main idea behind my VWAP trading strategy is trading pullbacks to VWAP.

Simply put – I wait for the price to move away from VWAP, and when it comes back to test it again, I anticipate that VWAP will work as either a Support or Resistance level. For example, as shown here:

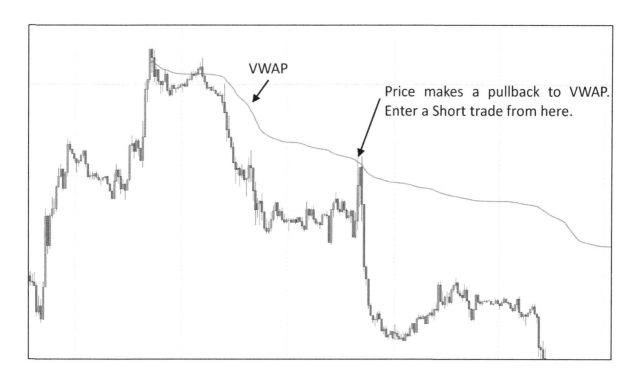

In the picture above, you'll notice a blue line - VWAP. When the price moves below this line and then retraces to test it, VWAP often acts as a Resistance level.

Why does this happen? It's because VWAP represents the trading position of an average trader, and many market participants use it as a reference point for their trade entries.

Imagine you want to enter a Short trade on the EUR/USD. The market is in a downtrend, and prices are dropping. Where's the best place to enter your Short position? It's not wise to enter randomly or at the current daily low. The logical entry point is where the average market participant sold, which is typically around VWAP. Institutional traders, the big players, follow a similar principle. In a hedge fund or a bank, supervisors might instruct traders to "Short X amount of lots on EUR/USD today, and do it at VWAP or better," with "better" meaning a price above VWAP.

When the price reaches VWAP, traders start entering their Short positions, causing the price to move away from VWAP once again. This is how markets operate and why VWAP often functions as a Support or Resistance zone.

Returning to the image above, when the price hit VWAP from below, aggressive sellers began opening their Short positions, leading to a downward movement in the price.

Until now, I've explained that VWAP represents an average market participant, but I haven't clarified over what time period this average is calculated. This is where it can get a bit tricky because it's your choice to determine that period.

If you set the VWAP's starting point at the beginning of the trading day, it will reflect the average trader's position since the start of that day.

The chart displayed above shows ES (S&P 500 futures) on a 5-minute timeframe. In this chart, you can see VWAP anchored at the beginning of the trading day, representing the average trader's position since the start of the day.

This particular VWAP, anchored at the start of the day, is commonly referred to as the "Daily VWAP" and is widely used in trading.

However, it's important to note that VWAP can be anchored in various ways. What all these anchoring methods share in common is their placement at crucial points in the market – points where market participants make crucial decisions, where sentiments shift, and the rules of the game change. These are the most critical locations to anchor your VWAP, as they provide valuable insights into how the average trader perceives the situation since those significant turning points.

First, let's provide you with a list of these crucial anchoring points, and then we'll delve deeper into each one of them for a better understanding.

The most important places to anchor the VWAP:

- Beginning of: Day, Week, Year
- Important swing point
- Start of a trend
- Strong macro news
- Heavy volume zone
- Gap
- Earnings

The strategy

The basic idea behind trading with Anchored VWAP is easy to understand. You just wait for the price to move away from the VWAP line, and when it touches the VWAP again, that's your signal to enter a trade.

<u>For a Long trade:</u>

If the price is above VWAP (meaning buyers are in control) and it comes back down to VWAP from above, that's when you enter a Long position as the price touches VWAP.

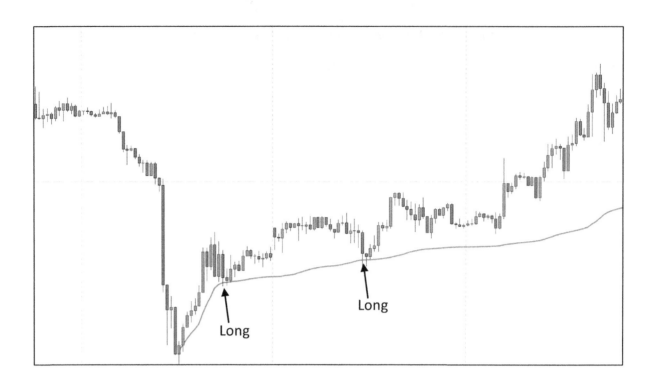

For a Short trade:

If the price is under VWAP (showing that sellers are in charge) and it comes back up to VWAP from below, that's your signal to enter a Short position as the price touches VWAP.

This is the most basic way to trade with VWAP. Personally, I like to see a bit more before making a trade, such as trade confirmation and alignment with other trading strategies. I'll explain these later, but for now, let's focus on the fundamentals so you don't feel overwhelmed right from the beginning.

Anchoring VWAP to dates

Start of the Day

This is the most traditional and widely used method of anchoring the VWAP.

When VWAP is anchored at the start of the trading day, it's referred to as the "Daily VWAP." Day traders, in particular, find this useful as they seek multiple trading opportunities throughout the day.

You can choose a time frame anywhere from 1-minute to 1-hour, but my personal preference for trading with the Daily VWAP is the 5-minute time frame.

The VWAP calculation begins at the start of the Asian trading session and concludes at the end of the US trading session.

Example #1 (Daily VWAP)

Take a look at this example of EUR/USD on a 5-minute chart with the Daily VWAP. You'll notice that for most of the day, the market stayed above the VWAP line, indicating that buyers were in charge.

At various points, the price came back to the VWAP line, which acted like a solid Support level, and the price responded well to it.

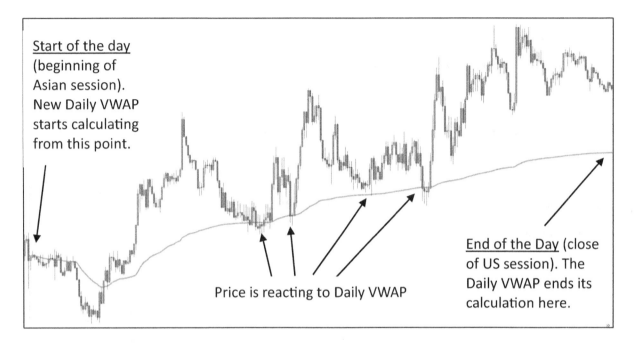

Start of the day (beginning of Asian session). New Daily VWAP starts calculating from this point.

Price is reacting to Daily VWAP

End of the Day (close of US session). The Daily VWAP ends its calculation here.

The image above displays the Daily VWAP, which begins during the Asian session and stops at the end of the US session. After that, I don't use this VWAP for trading anymore. Instead, I transition to trading with the new Daily VWAP that starts forming as the new Asian session kicks off.

Example #2 (Daily VWAP)

Let's look at an example on GBP/USD, using a 5-minute chart. The price spent most of the day above the Daily VWAP, indicating that buyers were in charge. Whenever the price pulled back to VWAP, it presented a potential opportunity for a Long trade, and buyers often took advantage of these chances to buy at VWAP.

When you're trading intraday with VWAP, it's important to understand that the price may not always react exactly when it touches the VWAP line. It might go a bit past VWAP before responding, and that's perfectly normal.

It can also happen for the price to simply pass by VWAP without any significant reaction. This is part of trading, as there's no strategy that works perfectly all the time.

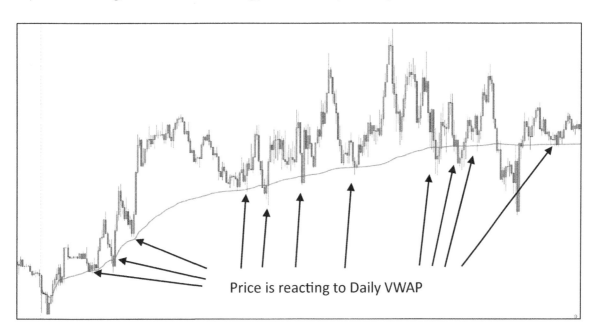

Price is reacting to Daily VWAP

Example #3 Daily VWAP

Take a look at this 5-Minute chart of GBP/USD. I want to show you how a "broken" VWAP can still be useful.

In this example, the first part of the day belonged to the buyers. The price was above VWAP, and whenever it touched VWAP, there was a reaction.

But then, something changed. The price broke through VWAP, turning what used to be a Support into a Resistance. What does this mean for us as traders?

Instead of seeking Long trades, we now search for Short trades. We want to see the price touch VWAP from below and go short from there.

However, if the price breaks above VWAP again, and the Buyers regain control, then we start looking for Long trades once more.

In simple terms, if the price is above VWAP, it acts as Support. If the price is below VWAP, it becomes a Resistance. This can happen several times in a day! Personally, I prefer when it doesn't happen too often and when markets are trending clearly in one direction, but in trading, things are rarely perfect.

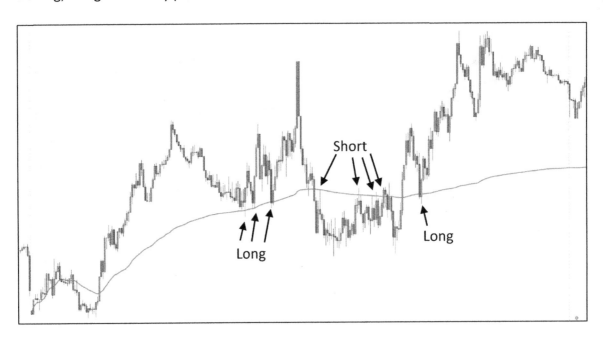

A VWAP that starts at the beginning of the trading week (at the start of the Asian Session on Monday) is known as the Weekly VWAP. It's one of my favorites, especially when I'm trading intraday with a 30-minute time frame.

I find it more effective than the Daily VWAP because, in my experience, it provides better trading signals. At least on the 30-minute time frame, which I prefer for intraday trading.

I always have the Weekly VWAP on my trading workspace, and I like to combine its signals with those from Volume Profile (we'll discuss this more later).

Now, let's look at a couple of trade examples using the Weekly VWAP.

Example #1 (Weekly VWAP)

Here's an example of a Weekly VWAP on a 30-minute chart for Gold. Gold prices have been falling all week, staying below the VWAP. This suggests that sellers were in control. There were a few times when the price went back up to the VWAP, and, except for the last one, each time it led to a successful reaction.

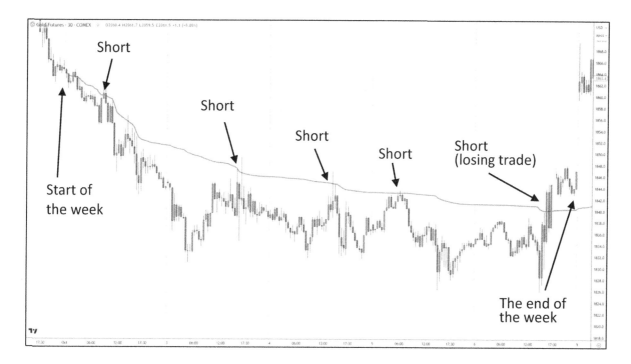

Based on my experience, VWAP performs exceptionally well in trending markets like this one, allowing us to use VWAP pullbacks as entry points in the direction of the trend.

Example #2 (Weekly VWAP)

Here's an example of Weekly VWAP on a 30-minute EUR/USD chart. Initially, buyers dominated, and we looked for Long trades when the price touched VWAP from above. However, a major news event shifted the market sentiment. The price quickly crossed below VWAP, turning VWAP into a Resistance. This Resistance level was tested on Friday.

Start of the year

A VWAP that begins on the first day of the year and ends on the last day is known as the Yearly VWAP. It's one of my top choices for swing trading or long-term trading, and I typically use it on a Daily timeframe (1 candle represents 1 day).

The Yearly VWAP helps us see how the average trader has been performing since the start of the year and where the "fair" price for the year is.

I always include the Yearly VWAP on my charts when analyzing swing trades. I like to combine it with my Volume Profile strategies (I'll explain more about that later).

Now, let's take a look at a few trade examples using the Yearly VWAP.

Example #1 (Yearly VWAP)

This is a Yearly VWAP on a Daily chart of Exxon Mobil stock. From the beginning of the year, the price has been above the Yearly VWAP, indicating that buyers have been dominating. The strategy is straightforward: wait for price pullbacks to VWAP and enter a Long trade when the price touches the VWAP line from above.

As you can see, VWAP is useful not only for forex trading but also for other types of instruments.

See how VWAP works well as a strong Support line. If the market wasn't in a trend, this strategy would be much more challenging to trade.

Example #2 (Yearly VWAP)

Sometimes, the trend is so strong and steep that the VWAP line stays far away from the current price most of the time, and trading opportunities come up only occasionally. This is the case in the example below, where there were only two instances of price pulling back to the VWAP.

The first reaction was excellent and allowed for trailing the short trade.

The second reaction might appear small, but remember, we're looking at a Daily timeframe, and in reality, it resulted in about a 200-pip movement.

As you might agree, having only two trades per year isn't too much. That's why I trade a variety of forex pairs, stocks, and other instruments, and I also use different trading strategies. If I focused solely on a few instruments and this strategy, I could easily end up with just a couple of trades for the entire year.

One of my favorite ways to use VWAP effectively is by anchoring it at key swing points in the market. These swing points are moments where the market sentiment shifted significantly, essentially changing the rules of the game. While there isn't an exact definition for these points, they are typically easy to spot once you're familiar with them, and practice will help you identify them on a chart.

These important highs and lows serve as pivotal decision-making points for traders. They are widely recognized and acted upon by majority of traders in the market, making them excellent reference points for anchoring VWAP.

In simple terms, think of a significant high or low as a crucial event that many traders in the market takes note of. VWAP then tells you whether the price is currently above or below the "fair" or "average" price since that game-changing moment, helping traders make informed decisions. Let's explore a couple of examples to illustrate this concept.

Example #1: VWAP anchored at swing point

In the example below, you'll see a 30-minute chart of S&P 500 futures. I chose to anchor the VWAP at the lowest point on the chart, which marked the pivotal moment when the downtrend reversed, giving way to an uptrend. This specific swing point is the ideal reference for anchoring your VWAP.

From that point onward, the price interacted with this anchored VWAP on three occasions, each time yielding a precise and favorable response. In all these instances, this VWAP acted as a reliable Support level.

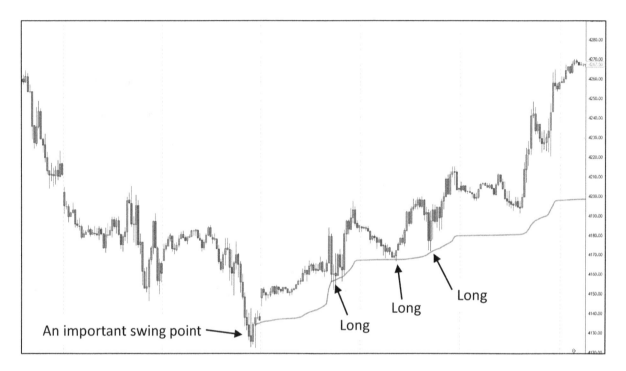

The great thing about anchoring VWAP at a swing point is that it works well with different timeframes in trading. You can find key swing points on a daily chart and use VWAP for daily swing trading. Or, you can use it for intraday trading on a 5-minute chart.

Just remember, if you analyze on a daily chart and anchor VWAP there, stick to trading on the daily time frame. Use Stop Loss and Take Profit levels suitable for that timeframe to keep your strategy consistent and effective.

Example #2: VWAP anchored at swing point

This is a daily chart of Apple stock. At the beginning of 2023, there was a significant low point (swing point). This marked the moment when a downtrend changed into an uptrend, a crucial event that influenced investors' decisions.

During the uptrend that followed, the price mostly remained above the VWAP, indicating that buyers were in control. However, when it eventually pulled back and touched the VWAP, something interesting happened. The VWAP acted as strong Support, and the price immediately responded to this Support level.

When the price hit the VWAP, it attracted buyers looking for a good price. Their aggressive buying activity helped push the price higher once again.

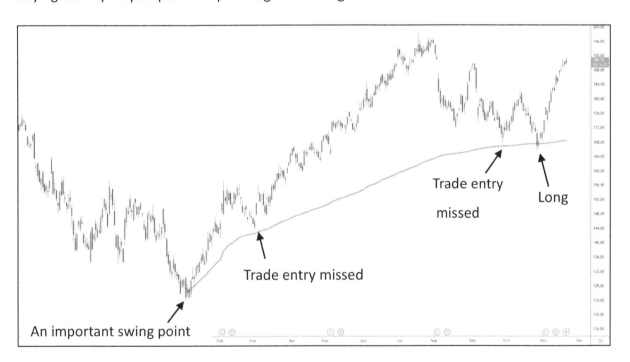

25

Example #3: VWAP anchored at swing point

This example is quite unusual because it involves a dramatic swing point. There was a sudden and large drop in the USD/JPY currency pair, which can happen unexpectedly with the JPY currency. However, this sharp drop was quickly reversed when aggressive buyers stepped in, causing the price to rise again. All of this price action resulted in a very noticeable and significant swing low, one that's hard to miss.

In such cases, it's a good idea to use the VWAP tool and anchor it at the candle that marked this strong low point. Later on, you'll see that the VWAP line drawn from this point acted as a Support level, and the price reacted to it multiple times. Below, you can see a 5-minute chart illustrating this.

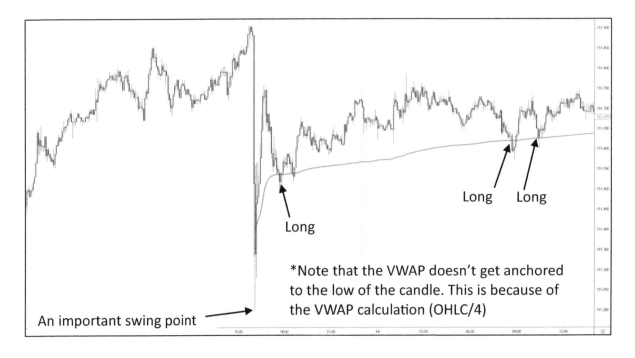

Long

Long   Long

*Note that the VWAP doesn't get anchored to the low of the candle. This is because of the VWAP calculation (OHLC/4)

An important swing point

Anchoring VWAP to start of the trend

Another crucial moment in trading is the beginning of a trend. When a strong trend emerges, every trader needs to adapt. Some want to find the perfect time to join the trend and jump in, while others, if the trend goes against them, seek a suitable exit point for their losing trades.

What both groups have in common is their desire to do this at the "fair" price, which is represented by the VWAP. The challenge here is pinpointing where the trend actually began. It can be somewhat subjective; two traders might choose different candles on the chart to anchor their VWAP. Typically, this doesn't lead to significant differences, and the VWAP provides similar Support and Resistance levels. However, if two traders anchor their VWAPs to candles that are too far apart, their VWAP lines may diverge more.

Here's how I do it: I consider a big candle near the point where the trend started as the starting point. The larger the candle, the more significant it is for me. Let's explore some examples to illustrate this concept.

Example #1: VWAP anchored to start of the trend

In the image below, you can see a 30-minute chart of S&P 500 futures, where a significant downtrend is beginning. This downtrend starts with a large red candle, and I decided to anchor my VWAP at this point. The trades in this example were straightforward because the price remained below the VWAP throughout (indicating that sellers were in control), and the VWAP consistently acted as a strong resistance, never failing even once.

Example #2: VWAP anchored to start of the trend

In this next example, we're looking at the NZD/USD currency pair on a 30-minute chart. This scenario is a bit more complex because there's a change in the trend. Initially, there was a downtrend, and the price had two significant reactions to the VWAP as resistance. But then, something interesting happened—the price surged above the VWAP line, transforming it from a Resistance into a new Support.

At this Support level, traders who were previously selling in the downtrend wanted to exit their trades at a "fair price" (which is represented by the VWAP). This desire to exit at a fair price played a key role in causing the price to react to this new Support level on two occasions.

Example #3: VWAP anchored to start of the trend

In this next example, we're looking at the DAX stock index on a daily chart. I want to show that the VWAP trading approach works for all types of trading instruments and timeframes.

The image below illustrates the beginning of a trend, marked by a strong and clear bullish candle. This is where I anchored my VWAP.

After anchoring it there, the VWAP consistently acted as a strong Support level. There were two good opportunities for trade entries from this point onward.

Example #4: VWAP anchored to start of the trend

In this final example, we're looking at Bitcoin on a 5-minute chart. There was a powerful and rapid upward movement, characterized by a massive green candle (which Bitcoin is known for on occasion). If you anchored the VWAP at this candle, it presented one good opportunity for a trade entry. Unfortunately, this new uptrend didn't last long. Two things occurred during the first pullback to the VWAP:

Buyers who wanted to join the rising market jumped in at what they considered the "fair price" (which is represented by the VWAP). This influx of buyers helped push the price higher.

Sellers who found themselves in an unfavorable position due to the sudden move needed to exit their trades. How did they do it? By buying, which is the action required to close a short trade. This also contributed to driving the price upward.

So, in this case, there are two factors that contributed to the price moving up from the VWAP.

Shortly after that, the VWAP line, which was acting as Support before, was broken, and sellers entered the market. When the price crossed below the VWAP, it transformed into a resistance. At this moment, the VWAP became a level where sellers wanted to sell (at a "fair price"), and buyers who saw that the uptrend was ending and wanted to exit their long positions did so at this point. That's why the VWAP worked as a Resistance in this case.

Many trading decisions are influenced by major macro news and important economic events. That's why I prefer to anchor the VWAP at the candle where significant and game-changing news was released.

There are two important things to keep in mind:

Firstly, you need to be able to identify which macro news is truly important. The easiest way to do this is by checking www.forex-factory.com, which uses colors to mark macro news events. Yellow indicates low-impact news, orange is medium-impact, and red is high-impact. I recommend using this strategy primarily for high-impact (red) news.

2:30pm		USD		Core CPI m/m				0.3%	0.2%	
		USD		CPI m/m				0.0%	0.0%	
		USD		CPI y/y				3.1%	3.2%	
7:01pm		USD		30-y Bond Auction					4.77|2.2	
8:00pm		USD		Federal Budget Balance				-290.5B	-66.6B	
10:45pm		NZD		Current Account				-12.25B	-4.21B	

Not all high-impact news events are equally strong in moving the market. For example, "Unemployment Claims" is marked as high-impact news but may not have a significant impact on the market. On the other hand, "Monetary Policy Statement" is extremely powerful news. Unfortunately, Forex Factory assigns them the same level of importance. So, don't anchor your VWAP at the candle where "Unemployment Claims" was released, but definitely anchor it where "Monetary Policy Statement" was released.

We want strong macro news that creates volatility and a significant shift in market sentiment. Here's a list of the most crucial news events that are likely to do just that and are ideal for anchoring VWAP:

- Rate decision and Minimum Bid Rate (including the following press conference)
- FOMC Meeting and Monetary Policy Statement (with the following press conference)
- CPI (Consumer Price Index)
- GDP (Gross Domestic Product)
- NFP (Non-Farm Employment Change)
- Unemployment Rate

- Speeches by the leaders of major economies discussing topics directly affecting their economy and currency.

The TradingView platform has a useful feature that displays strong macro news events below the chart, making it easy to find the candles associated with these events.

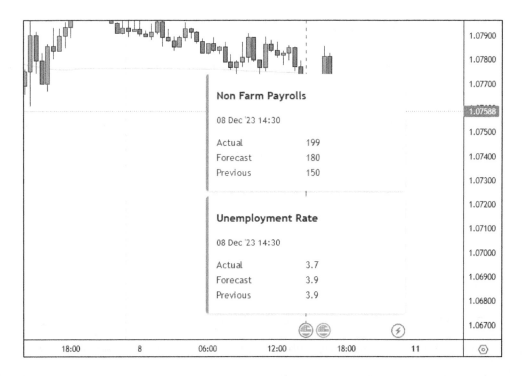

If you can't see this feature on your chart, you can enable it in the chart settings by selecting "economic events on the chart."

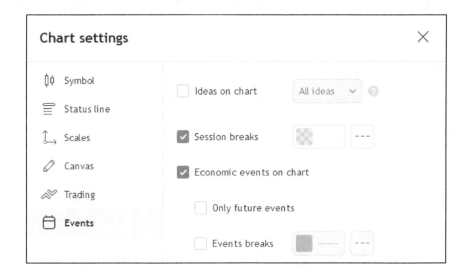

Secondly, it's essential to understand that even the most significant news may not always alter the market's mood. You're looking for macro news that kickstarts action, like a new trend. If the news only makes the price briefly jump up and down before settling back to its previous state, then it wasn't the game-changing news you were seeking (so, no need to anchor the VWAP there).

Here's an example of strong macro news that didn't impact the market sentiment:

Here's an example of an important macro news event that changed the market sentiment, making it a good choice to anchor your VWAP to:

In a nutshell, anchor your VWAP to candles that resulted from powerful macro news and led to significant market movements. This shows that the macro news was truly a game-changer, and other traders will base their decisions on this event.

I personally use this trading method for my short-term trades, which means I focus on timeframes ranging from 5 minutes to 30 minutes. Here are a few examples:

Example #1: VWAP anchored to macro news candle

In the chart below, you can see a 30-minute timeframe of the EUR/USD forex pair. This currency pair is greatly influenced by macro news from both the EU and US. One of the most impactful pieces of news is the Interest Rate Decision. This macro news has the potential to completely reshape trends and market sentiment, not only in the short-term for intraday trading but also in the long run.

In this case, the Interest Rate Decision sparked a fresh uptrend. I chose to anchor the VWAP at the candle corresponding to this significant macro news event. A few days later, the price retraced back to the VWAP, resulting in some favorable reactions and trade opportunities.

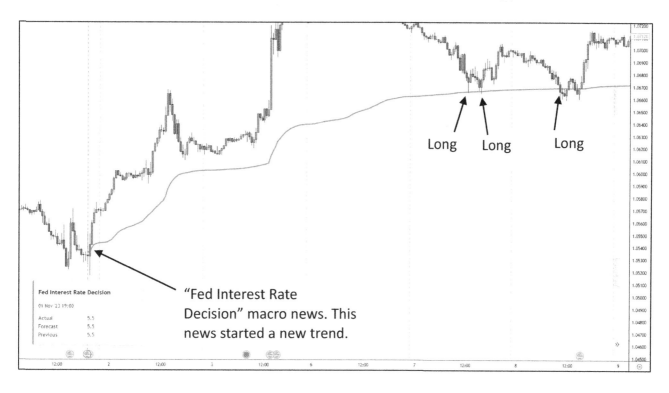

"Fed Interest Rate Decision" macro news. This news started a new trend.

Example #2: VWAP anchored to macro news candle

Here's an example on a 30-minute chart of USD/JPY. It shows a bullish candle caused by the "BoJ (Bank of Japan) Interest Rate Decision." This candle marked the beginning of a trend and was a definite game-changer. Shortly after, there was the first pullback to the VWAP, providing a great chance to join the trend and capture the momentum triggered by the macro news.

Later on, there were two more opportunities for long trades, but unfortunately, the momentum had faded. The price still reacted to the VWAP, but these were just quick in-and-out trades with no trailing.

When the price dropped below the VWAP, it then acted as resistance, offering a quick opportunity for a short trade.

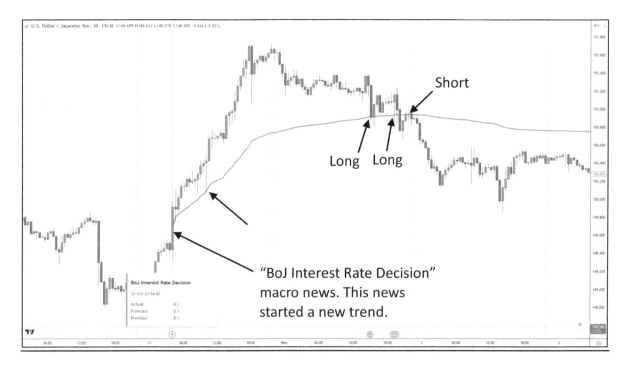

Heavy volume zones are crucial areas on a chart where large trading institutions have been actively placing many orders. These zones hold significant importance because it's these big players who have the ability to influence and even manipulate the markets.

To identify these heavy volume zones effectively, the best tool to use is Volume Profile. It's not a standard feature found in most trading platforms by default. You can obtain Volume Profile tools from my website at www.trader-dale.com or www.volumeprofile.com. My Volume Profile indicators are compatible with TradingView, NinjaTrader 8, and MetaTrader 4 platforms. They are user-friendly, extensively tested, and if you encounter any technical issues, our dedicated support team is available to assist you promptly.

Volume Profile can take on various shapes, and the one shown below is just one example:

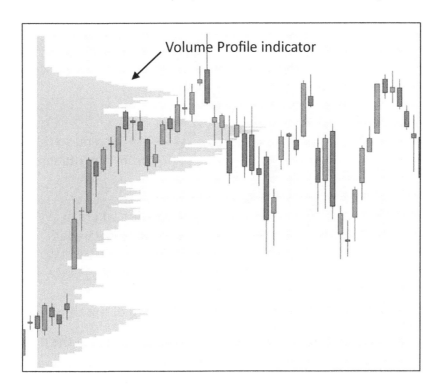

I use my Volume Profile indicator to identify heavy volume zones, typically found in areas where the price was consolidating. This is because major institutions prefer to slowly and discreetly accumulate their positions during these consolidation phases.

These rotation zones are usually followed by a clear trend, and this trend reveals the intentions of these large players:

If a rotation zone with heavy volumes is followed by an uptrend, it indicates that significant institutional buyers were quietly accumulating their long positions during the consolidation.

On the other hand, if a rotation zone with heavy volumes precedes a downtrend, it suggests that major institutional sellers were discreetly building their short positions during the consolidation.

The image below perfectly illustrates the scenario I prefer to trade. It shows a rotation zone with heavy volumes followed by a trend, indicating that strong institutional buyers accumulated their long positions in the consolidation zone and then drove (manipulated) the price upward.

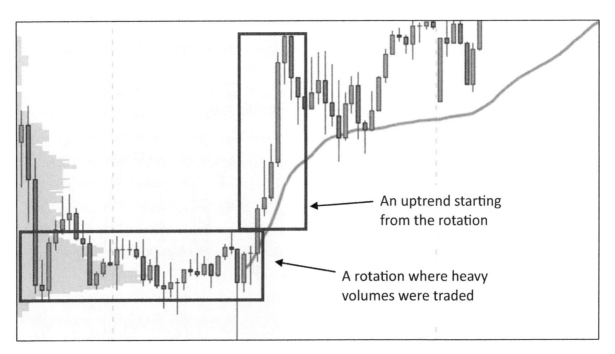

An uptrend starting from the rotation

A rotation where heavy volumes were traded

The trading approach here is to anchor the VWAP at the end of the consolidation zone, right where the trend begins. After that, you trade it as usual, jumping in at the pullbacks.

The beauty of this strategy is that it's applicable to any timeframe and any trading instrument. It's a universal approach that works whether you're looking at a 5-minute chart of EUR/USD or a daily chart of Tesla stocks. What's really great about Volume Profile and VWAP is their universality—the strategy remains the same regardless of the charts or instruments you use.

Now, let's dive into some examples to clarify things further!

Example #1: VWAP anchored to a heavy volume zone

This is a daily chart of Bitcoin. It shows a region on the chart where a lot of trading happened, and it looks like strong buyers were active in that area. They were slowly buying up Bitcoin for the long term.

When they really took charge and started pushing the price higher, it marked the beginning of an upward trend. This is the point where you should anchor the VWAP

As the price stayed above the VWAP, it meant that the buyers were in control. Then, there was a pullback, creating a good opportunity to enter a long trade and join the uptrend.

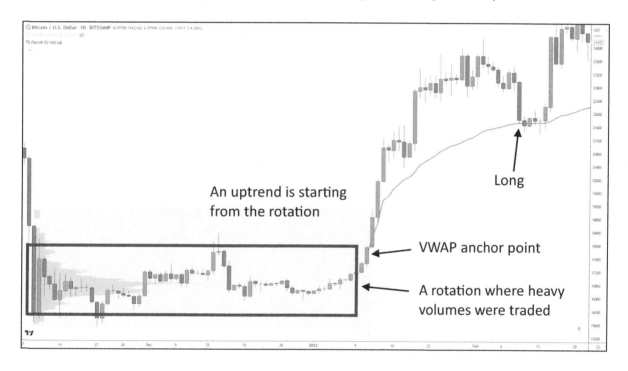

Example #2: VWAP anchored to a heavy volume zone

The image below displays a 30-minute chart of EUR/USD. You can see a rotation, and it's where a trend begins. To use the VWAP effectively, start at the beginning of this trend, which is the first large bullish candle. From this point, the market offers three chances to enter a good trade: look for price pullbacks to the VWAP during the uptrend.

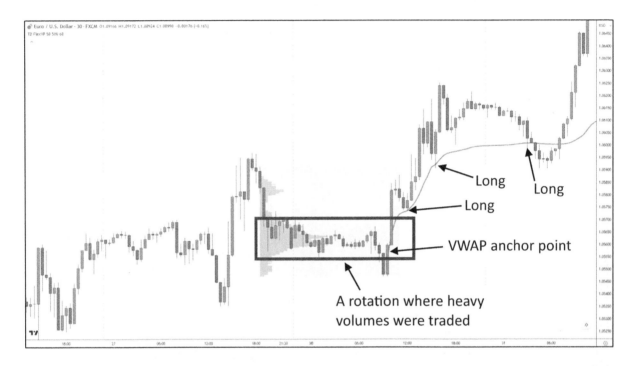

Example #3: VWAP anchored to a heavy volume zone

Below is a 30-minute chart of the S&P 500 index (futures). It shows a rotation zone where a lot of trading happened. During this time, big traders were accumulating their short positions. After that, the market started to drop in price, which means those big traders were selling aggressively.

To use the VWAP effectively, it's best to anchor it at the beginning of this drop. This is when you see the first big red candle that marks the start of the downtrend.

From that point on, the price kept staying below the VWAP line, indicating that the sellers were in control. During this time, there were three chances to enter at the pullback to the VWAP and sell along with these big traders.

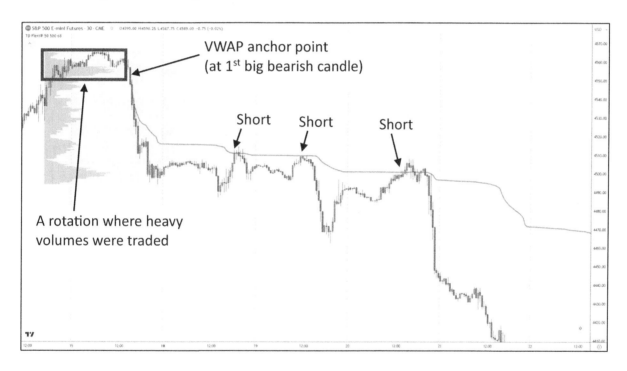

Volume Profile is a powerful trading tool that has various applications beyond VWAP. It can be used for institutional trading strategies, determining where to set Take Profit and Stop Loss, managing your positions, and more.

If you want to learn more about using Volume Profile effectively, I've written a book called "Volume Profile: The Insider's Guide to Trading." You can get a free download of the book at www.volumeprofile.com.

A gap occurs when the closing price of one candle is different from the opening price of the next candle. Gaps are more common in stocks because stock markets are not open 24/5 like some other instruments, such as currencies, which are traded continuously.

That's why this trading strategy primarily focuses on trading stocks. When it comes to the time frame, you have flexibility. You can use it for intraday trading, like on a 5 to 30-minute chart, or for long-term position trading with daily charts.

In either case, the key is to look for big gaps. These gaps are key points where many traders and investors base their decisions. When there's a big gap, everyone's attention is on it. Traders are assessing how their trades are performing compared to the average trade or, in other words, the fair price established after the significant gap. That's why a gap makes for a good anchoring point for the VWAP.

To implement this strategy, you need to analyze charts and identify these gaps. Then, you anchor the VWAP to the first candle after the gap, which is the opening candle. After that, you execute trades by looking for pullbacks to the VWAP, following the same approach as in the other trading scenarios we've discussed previously. Here are a couple of examples:

Example #1: VWAP anchored to a gap

The example below shows a 30 Minute chart of Apple stock. There is a big opening gap and VWAP is anchored to the first candle after the gap. The price is moving most of the time above the VWAP, reacting to it nicely.

Example #2: VWAP anchored to a gap

Here is a 5-minute chart of Procter & Gamble Company. Even though there was an opening gap on the upside, sellers quickly took over and pushed the price below the VWAP. This turned the VWAP into a Resistance level.

The opening gap was quite significant, and the price reacted to the VWAP multiple times.

Anchoring VWAP to earnings

Anchoring VWAP to earnings is a strategy that applies exclusively to stocks. It's somewhat related to our previous strategy where we anchored the VWAP to gaps. The reason for this connection is that the most significant and impactful gaps often happen right after earnings reports.

Here's how this strategy works: Start by opening a chart of the stock you want to trade and locate the earnings reports. If you are using the TradingView platform, this is quite straightforward, as earnings dates are displayed at the bottom of the chart. Anchor the VWAP to the point where the earnings report was released, and then trade pullbacks to the VWAP, following your usual approach.

You have the flexibility to apply this strategy on any time frame. I personally prefer the daily time frame, but you can also use it if you're an intraday trader, opting for shorter time frames like 5 or 30 minutes.

Here are a couple of examples to illustrate the concept:

Example #1: VWAP anchored to earnings

The chart below displays Meta stock on a daily time frame. After an earnings report, the day started with a significant gap. Since then, the buyers were leading the way, as the price consistently stayed above the VWAP line. Additionally, the price reacted each time it touched the VWAP.

There have been two more earnings reports after the one where I anchored the pullback. However, none of them resulted in such a substantial gap or surprised traders as much as this particular earnings report. That's why I consider this earnings report and gap to be much more significant than the others you can see on the chart.

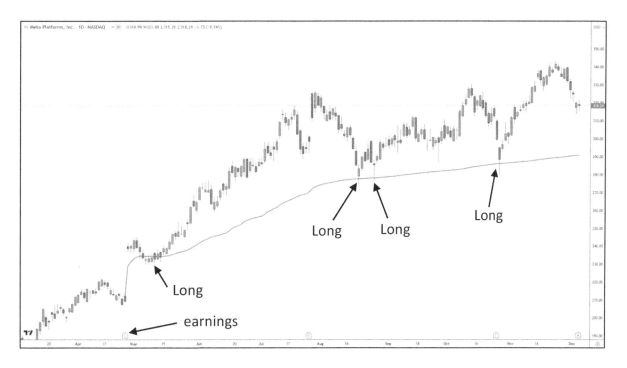

Example #2: VWAP anchored to earnings

The image below displays a 5-minute chart of Walmart stock. It's important to note that in a 5-minute time frame, the chart is more volatile compared to, let's say, a daily chart.

Following an earnings report, there was a big gap when the market opened. Once the initial volatility settled, the price mostly remained below the VWAP line. This suggests that even though the earnings news was positive, sellers had the upper hand, driving the price down.

After the initial volatility calmed down, there were three chances to enter a Short trade and make money on the downward movement.

Strategy #2: Reactions to 1ˢᵗ VWAP deviations

Until now, we've discussed strategies where the price responds to the VWAP line. Now, I'd like to introduce you to strategies that rely on VWAP standard deviations.

VWAP deviations, often referred to as "bands," consist of two lines positioned both above and below the VWAP line. These lines move alongside the VWAP and are calculated based on it.

The easiest way to make use of these deviations is to recognize whether the market is in a trend or a rotation. If the deviations are moving horizontally, it indicates that the market is in a **rotation**:

46

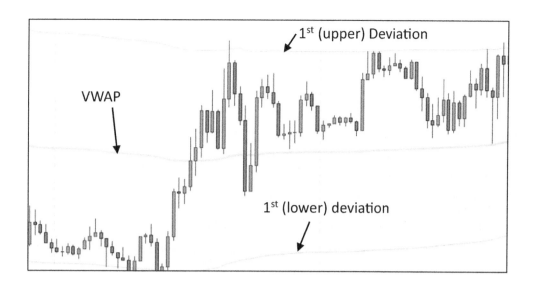

When the deviations move vertically, at least one of them, it signals that the market is in a **trend**:

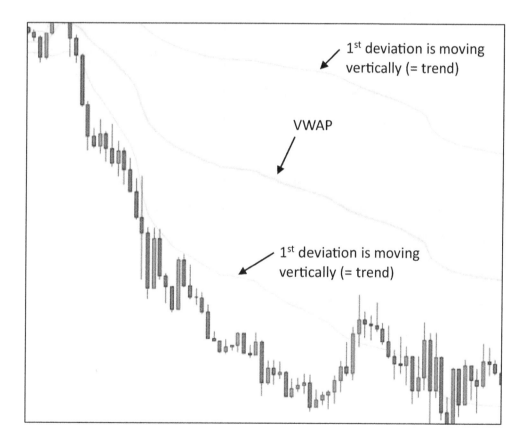

Distinguishing between a rotation and a trend using this method is user-friendly but not foolproof. While it's not flawless in every situation, it does provide valuable insights into the market's current state at a quick glance.

There are two strategies that rely on the 1st VWAP deviations. One is designed for trading in a market that is in rotation, while the other is tailored for trading in a trending market.

The setting

Before we delve into the two strategies, let me provide a quick note about the settings I use when trading with the 1st VWAP deviations.

I exclusively use the 1st deviations in conjunction with VWAP anchored to specific dates. This means VWAP anchored to the start of a day, week, or year. While it's not incorrect to use them with VWAP anchored to other reference points like swing points or trend beginnings, I find this approach to be the most practical and based on my real-world experience.

Additionally, I employ a unique color scheme for clarity. VWAP (anchored to a date) with deviations is depicted in yellow and grey, while Anchored VWAP without deviations is represented in blue. This visual distinction aids me in differentiating between the two.

Now, let's dive into the strategies!

VWAP Rotation strategy

This strategy is tailored for a market that is moving sideways, which indicates it's in a rotation phase. In this scenario, we need the 1st deviations to move horizontally.

When the market behaves like this, the price typically stays within the upper and lower 1st deviation lines. The upper 1st deviation acts as a Resistance level, while the lower 1st deviation serves as a Support level.

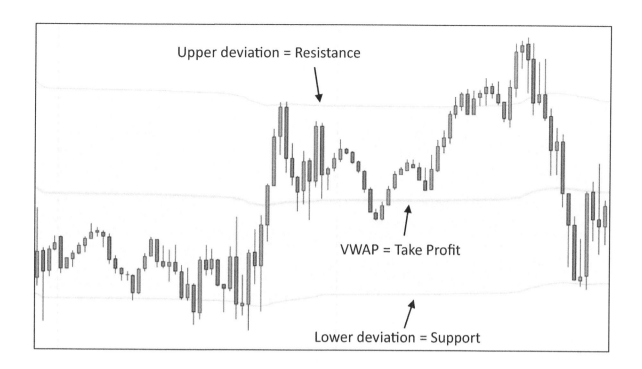

Upper deviation = Resistance

VWAP = Take Profit

Lower deviation = Support

Executing this strategy is quite straightforward

When the price touches the lower 1st deviation from above (acting as Support), enter a Long trade.

When the price touches the upper 1st deviation from below (functioning as Resistance), enter a Short trade.

For your Take Profit target, consider using the yellow VWAP line.

Time frame

For intraday trading, I opt for the Weekly VWAP, anchored to the start of the week, and use a 30-minute time frame. While Daily VWAP with a 5-minute time frame is also an option, I personally prefer the Weekly VWAP because it tends to be less volatile and provides what I consider more reliable trading signals.

For swing trading, I turn to the Yearly VWAP, anchored to the beginning of the year, and use a daily time frame.

It's important to emphasize that this strategy for a market that is in a rotation phase, meaning the price is moving sideways, and the 1st deviations are moving horizontally.

Example #1: VWAP Rotation strategy

The chart below illustrates S&P 500 futures using a 30-minute time frame. Initially, the 1st deviations are very close to each other, forming a tight channel. This is a typical occurrence, and it's essential to be patient as you wait for them to develop before trading with them.

At the beginning of the week, there was a trend in the market, making it unsuitable for this strategy. However, as the week progressed, the market transitioned into a rotation phase. Both deviations started moving sideways, and the price moved between them, creating the ideal conditions for this rotation-based strategy.

Once the price started to rotate, it responded nicely to the lower 1st deviation, presenting several opportunities for Long trade entries. Subsequently, there were two signals for Short trades (the second signal was less favorable as the price moved significantly beyond the deviation).

Finally, there was a signal for a Long trade.

For all of these trades, the VWAP was the ideal place to set your Take Profit target.

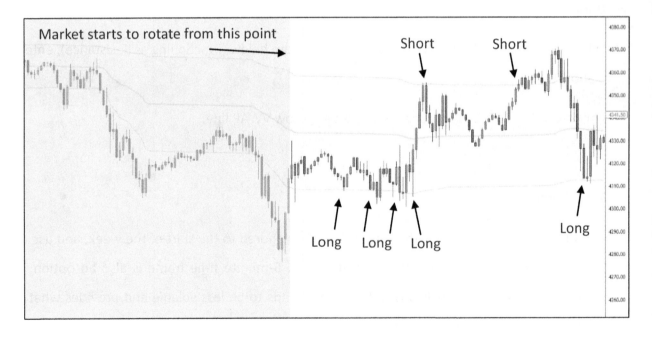

Example #2: VWAP Rotation strategy

The image below displays a daily chart of GBP/USD along with a Yearly VWAP anchored to the start of the year.

Initially, the market was in a trend, but later on, the deviations began to move sideways, and the market shifted into a rotation phase. Since then, there have been three opportunities for Long trades (although one trade did not work out as expected), and there have been two opportunities for Short trades.

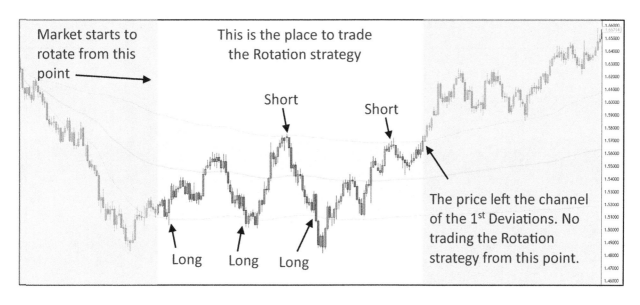

Example #3: VWAP Rotation strategy

The chart below shows USD/CAD on a daily time frame, with the Yearly VWAP plotted. Initially, the market was in an uptrend, but subsequently, it transitioned into a rotation phase, providing an opportunity to implement the VWAP Rotation strategy.

Since the rotation began, there have been two opportunities for Long trades and two opportunities for Short trades. However, once the price moved below the 1st deviation, it signified the end of the Rotation strategy and the beginning of the VWAP Trend strategy (which we will discuss further later).

This strategy is designed for a market that is in a trend. In such cases, the 1st deviations tend to move more vertically.

When the market is set like this, the price often remains either above the upper deviation or below the lower deviation.

For a Long Trade Scenario:

Look for the upper deviation to trend upward (moving vertically).

Confirm that the price is positioned above the upper Deviation.

Enter a Long trade when the price touches the upper deviation from above.

For a Short Trade Scenario:

Observe the lower deviation trending downward (moving vertically).

Verify that the price is situated below the lower Deviation.

Enter a Short trade when the price touches the lower deviation from below.

As this is a trend-based strategy, it offers the advantage of trading with a positive Risk Reward Ratio (RRR) and allows for trailing your Take Profit. The objective here is to enter a trend during a pullback and capture as much profit as possible!

Example #1: VWAP Trend strategy

Here's a 30-minute chart of S&P 500 index futures with a Weekly VWAP. Initially, it took some time for the Deviations to take shape, but it eventually became evident that the market was on an upward trend.

During this uptrend, every pullback to the upper deviation provided a viable opportunity for a Long trade entry.

Example #2: VWAP Trend strategy

This is a daily chart of GBP/USD with a Yearly VWAP. At the start of the year, the Deviations were too close to each other to trade, as they hadn't fully developed yet. However, a significant macroeconomic event occurred, leading to a significant price trend. It was during this period that the Deviations began signaling a trend, and the VWAP Trend strategy became feasible.

Following the strong sell-off, there have been three opportunities for Short trades.

Example #3: VWAP Trend strategy

Here's a daily chart of Oracle Corporation with a Yearly VWAP. Initially, as expected, the deviations were close together at the beginning of the year. However, as they started to develop, it became evident that the stock was in an uptrend.

Throughout the year, there were five chances to enter Long trades. Four of them turned out to be winners.

Confluences with other strategies

So far, we've covered some simple VWAP trading strategies that are solely based on VWAP itself. You can apply these strategies as I've demonstrated, and they tend to yield good results as they've been thoroughly battle-tested. However, because these strategies are relatively simple, they may not always produce consistent outcomes. There will be times when you receive multiple trading signals, and each of them turns out to be a winner, but there will also be cases where the price doesn't react to the VWAP or its Deviations, leaving you questioning whether the strategy has stopped working or if something is amiss.

In the long run, these strategies can provide favorable results, but if you're seeking greater consistency and a higher win rate, I recommend combining VWAP setups with other unrelated trading setups. This is the approach I personally follow, and it has delivered the best results for me.

I prefer to combine VWAP with Volume Profile and Price Action setups. When two or more independent trading setups align to point to the same Support or Resistance level, I refer to it as a "confluence". These confluences provide strong zones to trade from.

Now, I'll introduce you to my most favored Price Action and Volume Profile setups, and then we'll combine them with VWAP setups. It might seem a bit complicated, but don't worry, it's not as complex as it appears. Once you grasp this approach, you'll be amazed by the results it can achieve!

Price Action setup: Support becomes Resistance (and vice versa)

This is one of my favorite Price Action strategies, and I usually spot this setup in the charts nearly every day, offering numerous trading opportunities.

This setup can work in both directions, where Support turns into Resistance and vice versa. Here's how to identify and trade it:

Start by observing the price strongly reacting or sharply moving away from a particular level on the chart. This strong reaction signifies the presence of strong Support or Resistance in that area, and the market is responding to it.

While one significant reaction is enough, it's even better if there are two or more strong reactions around the same area.

After identifying such a strong zone, wait for the price to go through it. You want to see the price break through this strong Support or Resistance level.

Despite breaching the level, this level remains significant and strong. The reason is that breaking such a Support or Resistance demands a substantial push, involving a considerable amount of strength and trading volume from either strong buyers or sellers. When the price revisits this zone, it tends to be defended because it was a crucial level in the past. This is how Support can become Resistance and vice versa.

Once you've identified a Support becoming Resistance (or Resistance becoming support) level, wait for the price to return to this level, and that's when you enter your trade.

This setup is effective across various timeframes. Personally, I prefer to look for it on daily and 30-minute charts.

Although it may seem like there are six somewhat complex and possibly confusing steps to explain, I'll provide you with a few examples, and I'm confident everything will become crystal clear!

Example #1: Support becomes Resistance (and vice versa)

While I'm writing this, I just executed a trade based on the same concept – what a nice coincidence! Allow me to walk you through what I did.

Here's a 30-minute chart of NZD/JPY. There was a zone on the chart where the price had strongly bounced off twice in the past. This suggests that in the past, it served as a strong Resistance level. However, this Resistance level was breached, transforming it into a new Support level.

All I had to do was wait until the price revisited this zone, and that's when I entered a Long trade.

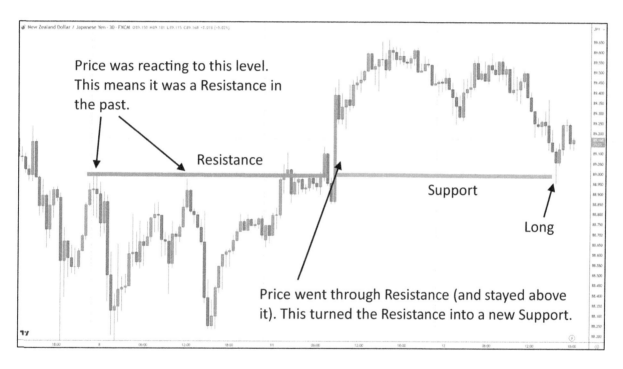

This illustrates the Long trade scenario of this setup, where a previously breached Resistance level becomes a new Support. Additionally, there was another setup that further reinforced this Support, which was a Volume Profile setup, but I'll delve into that later on.

Example #2: Support becomes Resistance (and vice versa)

Here's a 30-minute chart of S&P 500 futures. The price made strong reactions in the area of the red level I've highlighted in the image. To be precise, it wasn't necessarily hitting the exact level, but rather the area around it. That's because Supports and Resistances are not precise points; they represent zones.

Therefore, the price's strong reactions to this zone indicated that the market considered it as a Resistance. However, once this zone was breached, it turned into a new Support level, presenting a nice opportunity for a Long trade.

Example #3: Support becomes Resistance (and vice versa)

Here's another example from the daily chart of Bitcoin. The price made multiple reactions to the red zone I've highlighted in the image. This recurrent behavior indicated that the zone served as a strong Resistance level. However, once the price decisively broke through this Resistance and remained above it, the zone turned into a new Support.

Later on, this newly formed Support level was tested, presenting a good opportunity to enter a Long trade.

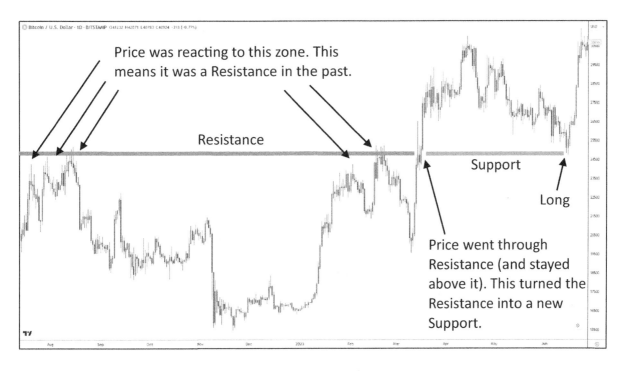

Example #4: Support becomes Resistance (and vice versa)

The final example is a 30-minute chart of EUR/USD, and it presents a reverse scenario compared to what I've previously shown.

In this case, the price rebounded from the green line, forming a significant daily low. This action indicated that the market considered this level as strong support. However, the following day, during a macroeconomic news release, this Support was breached, turning it into a new Resistance.

This illustrates the Short trade scenario of the setup, where a previously breached Support level becomes a new Resistance.

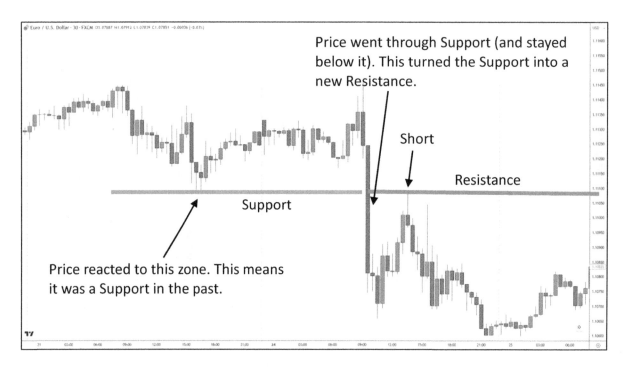

Volume Profile Trend setup

I have several Volume Profile setups that I enjoy trading, and I've detailed them comprehensively in my Volume Profile trading book. However, there's one particular setup, the Volume Profile Trend Setup, that pairs exceptionally well with VWAP.

I say it works best because VWAP setups tend to excel in markets that are trending (except for the VWAP rotation setup). My Volume Profile Trend Setup is specifically designed for use in trending markets. This is why I seek instances where these two setups align, indicating the same Support or Resistance level, and use them as trade signals.

Now, let me clarify how the Volume Profile Trend Setup works.

Volume Profile trend setup explained

I use the Trend Setup when the market is in a strong trend. A strong trend means that either buyers or sellers are more aggressive compared to the other side. In an uptrend, it's aggressive buyers pushing the price up, while in a downtrend, it's aggressive sellers driving it down.

When you look at the volumes traded in a trend, you'll usually see that Volume Profile is rather thin. That's because trends move quickly, and there isn't enough time for big players to accumulate their positions.

But within a trend, there are moments when the price takes a breather and slows down a bit. During these pauses, traders and investors have a chance to add to their positions. These moments create what we call a "volume vluster" within the trend. It's important that this volume cluster forms within the ongoing trend, indicating that aggressive market participants are adding to their existing positions.

Long trade scenario:

If a volume cluster forms within a strong uptrend, it suggests that buyers were adding more to their Long positions as the price moved higher. If the price retraces to the volume cluster, it's likely to find support there and continue moving higher. In an uptrend, we consider the volume cluster as a Support level, and I prefer to enter my trades at the beginning of this volume cluster.

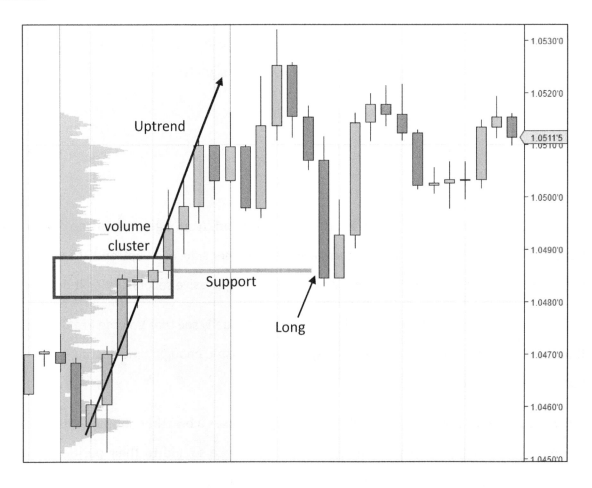

Short trade scenario:

If a volume cluster forms within a strong downtrend, it suggests that sellers were adding more to their Short positions there as the price was falling. If the price retraces to the volume cluster, it's likely to encounter resistance at that level and continue moving downward. In a downtrend, we view the volume cluster as a Resistance point, and I prefer to enter my trades at the start of this volume cluster.

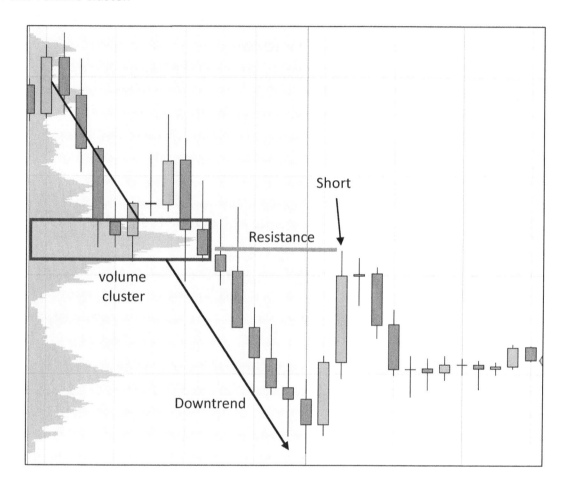

Now that we've covered the theory, let's delve into a few practical examples!

Example #1: Volume Profile Trend setup

Here's a 30-minute chart of ES (S&P 500 futures). It's in a strong downtrend, which means we're hunting for important volume clusters within this trend to take Short trades.

On this chart, there are two notable volume clusters that have formed during the downtrend. The first one has already been tested, and the price responded well to it.

The second volume cluster, however, hasn't been tested yet. It acts as an active Resistance level, and if the price reaches it, we expect a reaction.

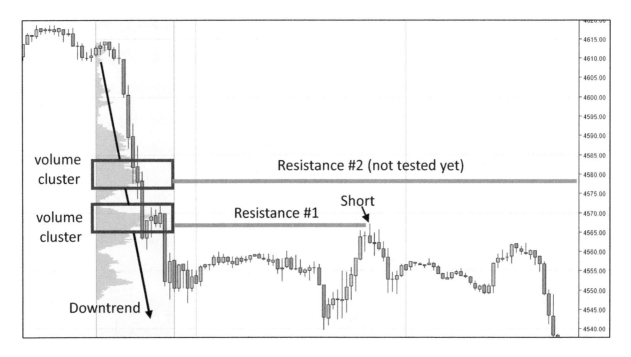

Example #2: Volume Profile Trend setup

The image below displays a 30-minute chart of GBP/USD. During an uptrend, three important volume clusters appeared. When the price retraced and tested each of them, they all acted as expected, and the price bounced off them nicely.

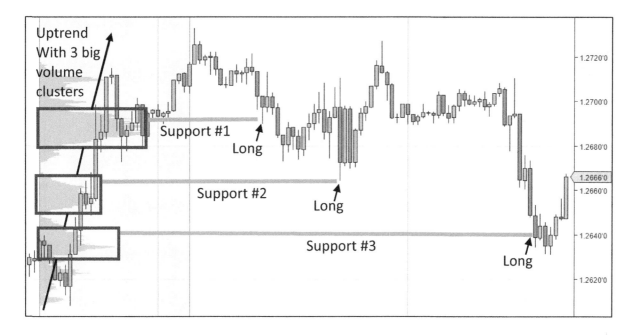

Example #3: Volume Profile Trend Setup

In the next example, you'll see a daily chart of NZD/USD. This chart displays a strong downtrend where two significant volume clusters were created. As time went on, the price retraced to these volume clusters, and it responded positively when it reached them.

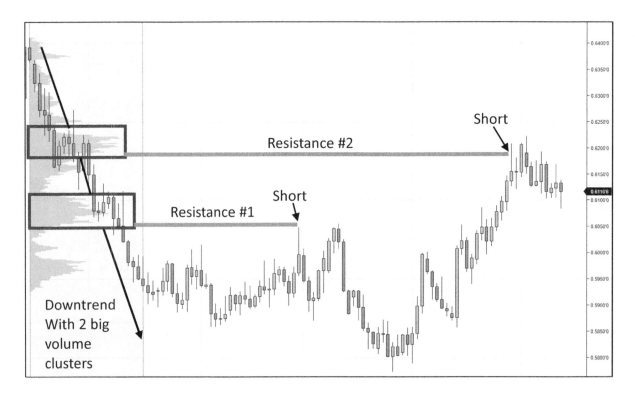

Combos of multiple trading setups

So far, we've learned about these individual trading setups:

- Anchored VWAP (anchored to important dates, swing points, start of trends, macro news candles, heavy volume zones, gaps, earnings)
- Trading with 1st VWAP Deviations
- Price Action setup
- Volume Profile setup

Now, I'll show you how to combine these setups to identify very strong Support and Resistance zones. Combining these methods often results in more consistent and effective outcomes compared to using each one individually.

The process is straightforward. You examine a chart and search for areas where two or more trading strategies indicate a Support or Resistance level. For instance, if both the Anchored VWAP and Volume Profile setups highlight the same level (or very close), the likelihood of that level being significant increases compared to when only one strategy identifies it.

Keep in mind that these setups don't have to align precisely at the exact level, but if they converge within the same general area, it can be considered a confluence. Let me clarify with a couple of examples.

Example #1: Multiple setups combo

Here's a daily chart for Mondelez International, where we're combining two trading strategies: VWAP and Volume Profile. The VWAP is anchored to the day when earnings were reported, making it an important point of reference. When the price moves away from the VWAP, it tends to come back for a retest.

What's especially interesting here is that during this pullback to the VWAP, there's also a Volume Profile Trend Setup lining up with this level. In simple terms, both indicators are pointing to the same Support level. This alignment of two independent trading strategies makes this level even more significant and increases the likelihood of a successful price reaction.

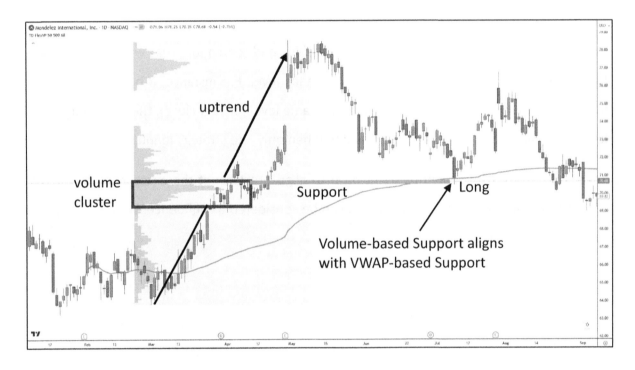

Example #2: Multiple setups combo

Let's check out Bitcoin's daily chart, where we're using two good trading strategies – VWAP and Volume Profile. We've set the VWAP based on a strong volume zone that appeared just before a significant uptrend.

At first, the price was above the VWAP, indicating strong buyer interest. But later on, it dropped and came closer to the VWAP, making a pullback.

What's intriguing here is that during this pullback, another Support level popped up thanks to the Volume Profile Trend Setup, which focuses on trading volume clusters. When both of these setups highlight the same Support level, it becomes a robust Support zone.

In simpler terms, when two strategies agree on a level, it becomes a strong level with a better chance of a successful reaction.

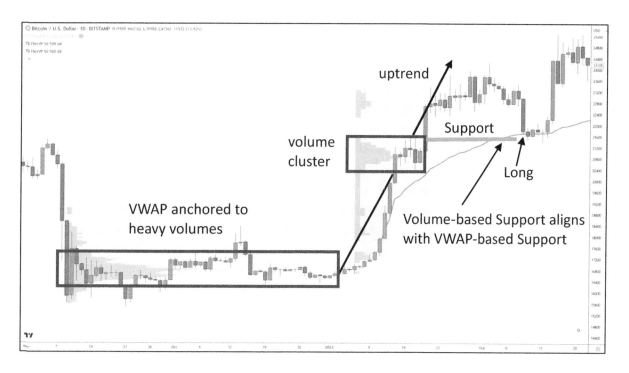

Example #3: Multiple setups combo

Let's take a look at this 5-minute chart for S&P futures (ES). We're using two trading strategies here – VWAP and Price Action.

At the start of the day, the price was moving around the VWAP without a clear direction. But later on, it took a significant drop below the VWAP, signaling that the sellers were taking control.

Now, when the price made a pullback to the VWAP, something interesting occurred. The Price Action setup also indicated a broken Support level, which had now become a new Resistance level.

To put it simply, two different strategies were both pointing out the same thing – there was a strong Resistance zone at that level. This made it a good signal for a short trade.

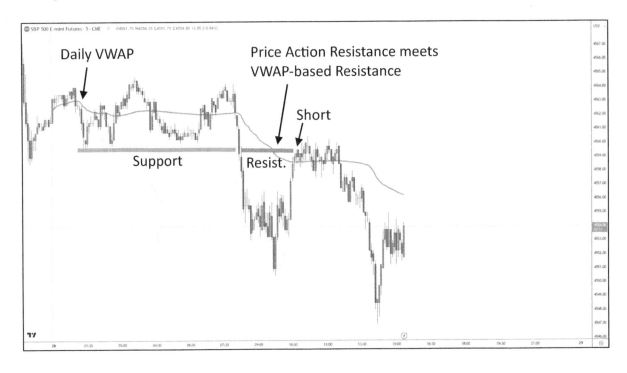

Example #4: Multiple setups combo

Let's take a look at this daily chart of GBP/USD, where we're using two trading strategies – VWAP and Price Action.

The VWAP was initially set at the start of the year, representing the Yearly VWAP. In the beginning, the price was moving in a narrow range. But then, there was a sudden drop, signaling the start of a new trend.

After this drop, we had a good opportunity for a Short trade when the price retraced to the 1st deviation from below. While this trade relied solely on the VWAP strategy and didn't involve multiple setups, it still had potential.

However, the second test was even more interesting. This is where the Price Action strategy came into play. It highlighted a broken Support level that had turned into a Resistance level. When both of these setups pointed to the same Resistance zone, it became an excellent point to enter a Short trade.

Example #5: Multiple setups combo

Let's check out Tesla's daily stock chart, where we're using two trading strategies – VWAP and Price Action.

Think of VWAP like an average yearly price. In the beginning of the year, the price was above VWAP, suggesting that buyers were in charge. Initially, there were two opportunities to consider a Long trade when the price pulled back.

However, the third pullback was more interesting. This time, it aligned perfectly with another strategy – Price Action. This approach identified a previous Resistance level that had now turned into a Support level.

What made this Support level special was that it matched with the Yearly VWAP. When two different strategies point to the same level, it creates a strong signal. And as you can see on the chart, the price reacted positively to it.

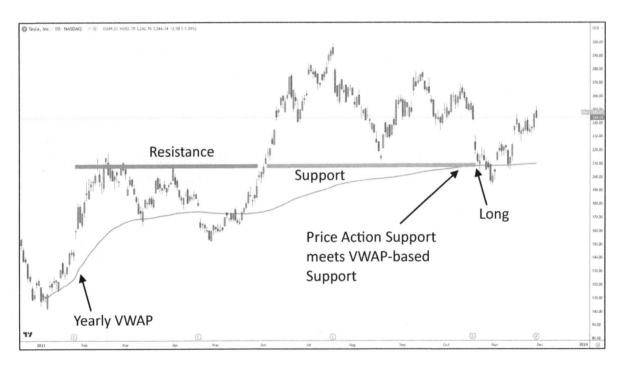

Example #6: Multiple setups combo

Take a look at Pfizer's daily stock chart, where we're using two trading strategies based on Anchored VWAP.

The first VWAP, called the Yearly VWAP, starts from the beginning of the year. It didn't have much impact on the price until it aligned with the second VWAP.

The second VWAP is anchored at a significant high point in the chart.

As these two VWAPs moved closer together, they created a powerful Resistance zone. When the price retraced or pulled back to this zone, it triggered a positive response.

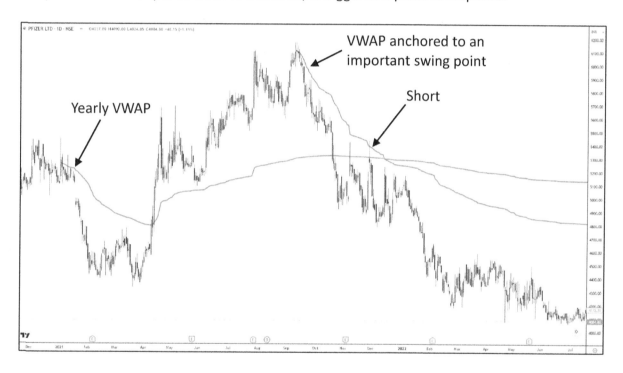

Trade entry confirmation

There are several methods to determine whether to enter a trade when it touches VWAP or not. Let's go through them one by one and discuss their advantages and disadvantages:

Entering a trade at first touch

This approach is the riskiest, especially if you solely rely on VWAP setups without any other supporting strategies.

In simple terms, you enter a trade as soon as it touches the VWAP line, without any confirmation.

This means you trade every signal blindly.

Using this method, you'll have the most trades, but your results won't be consistent. Yes, there will be times when almost every trade is a winner, leading to winning streaks. However, there will also be times when you'll face losses, question the strategy, and have a tough time. Your results won't be reliable.

Consistency is crucial in trading because it allows you to have more confidence in your strategy and gradually increase your trade sizes.

I do not recommend trading this way. While it's the easiest, it's also the riskiest. As traders, we must control our risks, and this approach doesn't provide that.

Entering a trade at first touch – with combos of multiple setups

Entering a trade as soon as the price touches VWAP can be risky. However, it's a different story when you have a combination of multiple independent trading setups aligning together. This is much more reliable!

Personally, I don't have any issues with entering a trade at first touch if the price reaches a level that's a strong Support or Resistance indicated by multiple trading setups. These signals are extremely strong, and the success rate is much more consistent.

So, if you want to trade at first touch, go for it, but make sure you're using these kinds of powerful combinations.

Entering a trade after a successful reaction

Confirming your trade entry by observing how the market reacts to a level is a proper and logical approach. It's a straightforward way to ensure you're making the right move. Here's how you can do it:

1. When the price reaches your Support or Resistance level, take the time to watch how it responds.

2. If the price does react to the level, meaning it bounces off it as expected, that's your signal to enter the trade.

3. I recommend waiting for one positive candle to show that the price is indeed reacting to the level. When that candle closes, and a new one opens, it's time to execute your trade.

4. For a long trade entry from a VWAP-based support, look for one bullish candle to close ABOVE the Support level.

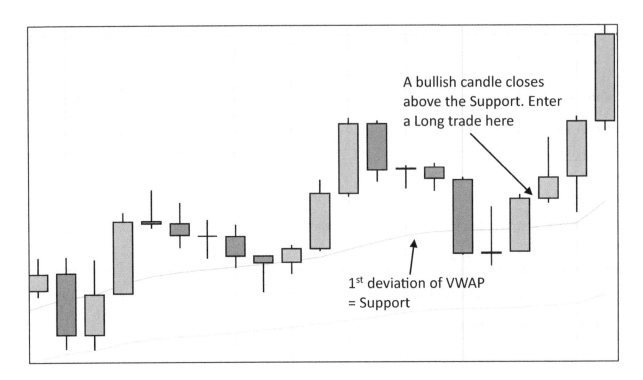

5. For a short trade, watch for a bearish candle to close below the Resistance level.

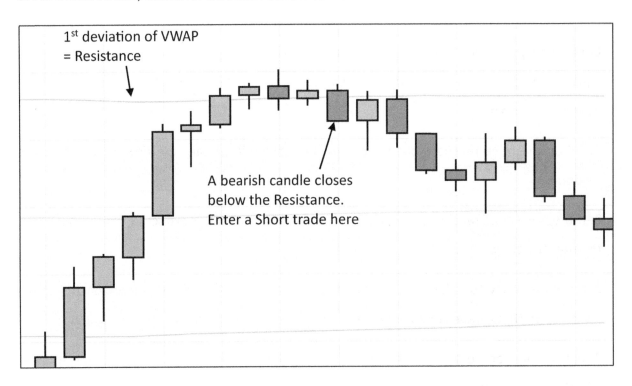

Observing these candlestick patterns and reacting accordingly provides a reliable confirmation for your trade entries.

Stop loss placement:

One advantage of this approach is that it provides a clear and effective location for placing your Stop Loss. You should position your Stop Loss behind the swing point of the market's reaction, which I refer to as the "Reaction Point." This method ensures that you always have a well-defined Stop Loss placement.

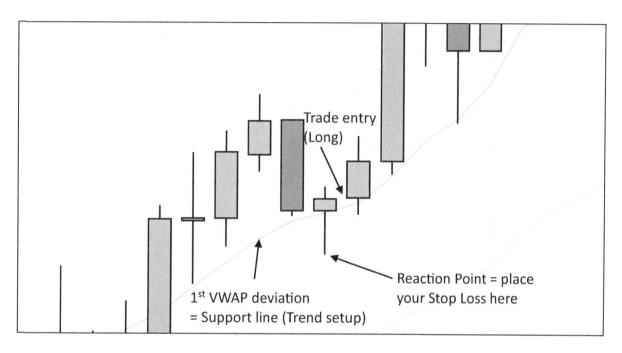

Trade entry (Long)

1st VWAP deviation = Support line (Trend setup)

Reaction Point = place your Stop Loss here

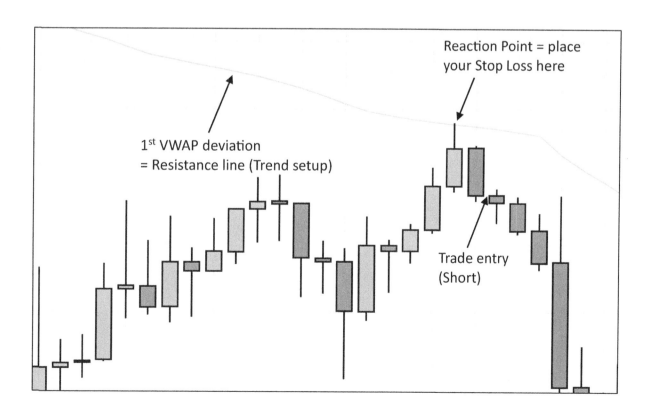

Reaction Point = place your Stop Loss here

1st VWAP deviation = Resistance line (Trend setup)

Trade entry (Short)

Disadvantage: missing out

One potential drawback of this approach is that you might miss out on some of the initial reaction because you enter the trade later. However, the benefit is that you can be more confident that the market is indeed reacting to the level. It's a trade-off between entering a bit late but with better confirmation.

The most frustrating situation you might encounter is when the confirming candle is very large, causing you to miss a significant part of the expected move. Unfortunately, there isn't much you can do about this, and you'll need to accept that it can happen occasionally.

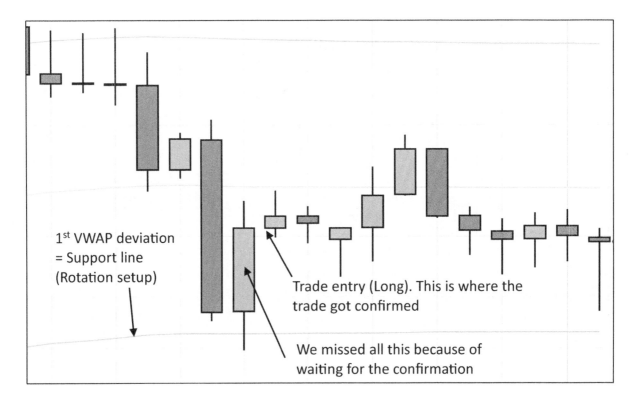

1st VWAP deviation = Support line (Rotation setup)

Trade entry (Long). This is where the trade got confirmed

We missed all this because of waiting for the confirmation

Time frame

I recommend sticking to a single time frame when using this confirmation method. For instance, if you are working with 30-minute charts, you should look for a bullish 30-minute candle closing above the Support for a long trade confirmation, not a different time frame like a 5-minute candle. Consistency within the same time frame you initially analyzed is a safer approach.

If you want to be more aggressive, you can switch to a slightly faster time frame for confirmation, but I advise against drastic changes. For example, if your initial analysis is on a 30-minute time frame, consider confirmation on a 15-minute time frame (a very aggressive approach would be on a 5-minute time frame).

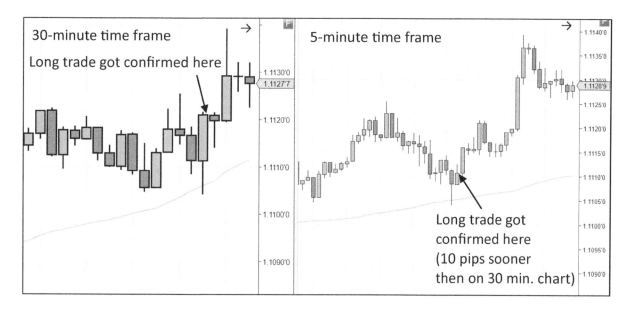

Order Flow confirmation

My preferred method for confirming trade entries is using Order Flow analysis. It's the most advanced approach and requires Order Flow software and knowledge of how to use it. However, once you master it, this method can become your favorite way to confirm trades.

Order Flow analysis displays all executed orders in the market, allowing you to track the actions of major trading institutions that influence and manipulate markets. You can see where these significant players are placing their large orders.

For example, if the price reaches a VWAP-based support, and you observe a sudden surge in activity by major players around that level (with significant volumes being traded), it serves as a strong confirmation that these institutions recognize the Support and are interested in trading it. Order Flow enables you to follow institutional traders' actions and trade alongside them, rather than against them.

There are numerous Order Flow strategies and confirmations you can use, but this book provides only a brief introduction. If you wish to explore Order Flow analysis further and receive proper training, you can visit www.orderflow.com.

Here are a couple of examples of how to use Order Flow to confirm trade entries:

Example #1: Order Flow trade entry confirmation

One of my favorite confirmations using Order Flow analysis is called "Absorption." In the example below, you can see the price rising when suddenly there are significant volumes on both the Bid (left) and Ask (right) sides of the Order Flow footprint.

This situation indicates that buyers are aggressively trying to push the price up (visible on the Ask side, or the right side of the footprint), but at the same time, sellers are also selling aggressively, as evidenced by the large orders on the Bid side (left side of the footprint). Essentially, the sellers are absorbing the buying pressure.

When you observe this type of confirmation, known as absorption, occurring around a Support or Resistance zone (such as one created by VWAP), it suggests that the price is likely to reverse.

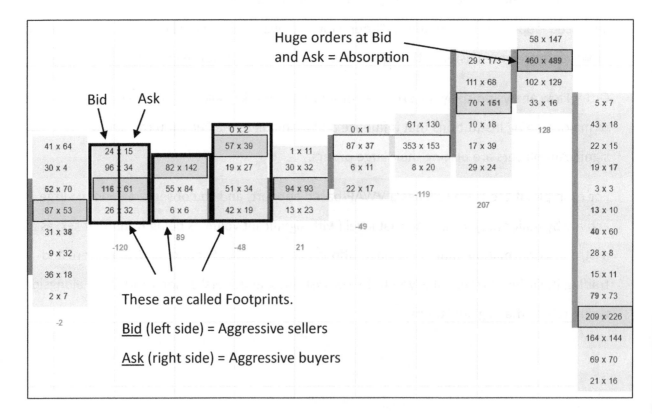

Example #2: Order Flow trade entry confirmation

The example below illustrates another type of Order Flow confirmation, known as "Limit Order" confirmation.

In this scenario, you're looking for a significant order to appear near your Support or Resistance zone, typically representing a Limit order placed by a major market participant, possibly a large institutional trader.

In the image, you can see the price suddenly surging upwards, followed by the appearance of a huge order of 353 contracts on the Ask side of the footprint. If this occurs around a robust Resistance zone, there's a good chance that this significant order was a Sell Limit order.

In simple terms, a significant player was waiting at this Resistance level, and when the price reached it, they initiated a pending Short trade.

This type of confirmation is valuable when considering whether to take the trade or not. It provides a clear signal that the level is being recognized by a major institutional trader, and the price is expected to react to it.

Note: A Limit Sell order appears on the Ask side, while a Market Sell order appears on the Bid side of the order flow footprint.

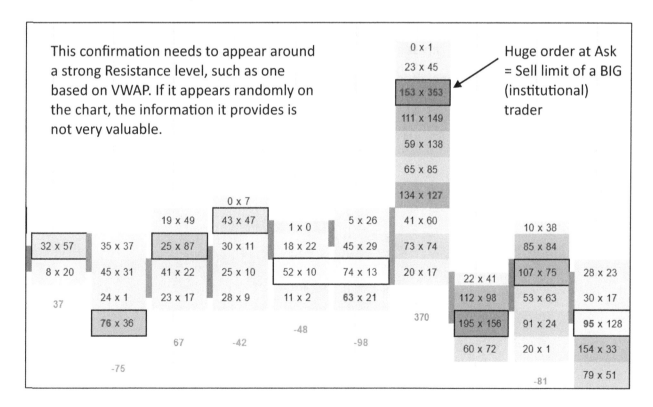

Example #3: Order Flow trade entry confirmation

The chart below displays a 1-Minute chart (represented by the black line), and below it, the green line represents a Cumulative Delta chart. While not exactly an Order Flow chart, Cumulative Delta provides information derived from the Order Flow (and it's also a part of my custom-made order flow software).

Cumulative Delta essentially illustrates the difference between bid and ask, which boils down to the distinction between aggressive buyers and sellers. When Cumulative Delta rises, it indicates that aggressive buyers are in control, whereas a decline suggests that aggressive sellers are taking the lead.

I use this chart to compare price movements with Cumulative Delta. Most of the time, these two charts move in sync, following the same direction. However, there are instances of divergence when the price moves differently from Cumulative Delta.

These divergences catch my attention. Why? Because, typically, the price tends to align with Cumulative Delta, and when a divergence occurs, it often signals that the price will soon change course to follow the Delta.

When I spot such a divergence, especially around a significant Support or Resistance level (like one based on VWAP), I consider it a strong confirmation that encourages me to enter the trade.

In the picture below, you can see a moment when the price is decreasing while Cumulative Delta is on the rise. Not long after this, the price changes its direction to align with the Delta.

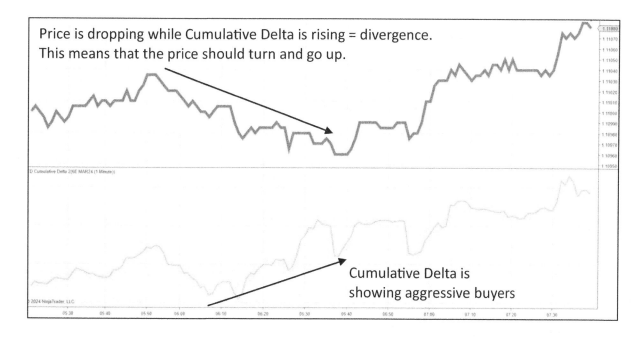

Price is dropping while Cumulative Delta is rising = divergence. This means that the price should turn and go up.

Cumulative Delta is showing aggressive buyers

Keep in mind that a divergence is a strong signal for a trend change, but it's most effective when the price is close to a strong Support or Resistance area, such as a VWAP-based Support or Resistance zone. This is when it works best.

Take Profit placement

There are several methods for determining where to place your Take Profit in trading, and they all share a fundamental rule that applies not only to VWAP but also to Volume Profile, Order Flow, or simple Price Action trading.

Here's the rule: Always exit your trade a bit before it reaches a significant barrier which could prevent the price moving further. These barriers are strong Support or Resistance levels identified through Price Action, VWAP, or Volume Profile analysis.

I use this approach because when the price approaches such a barrier, there's a risk that it might react and reverse at that Support or Resistance. I prefer to exit my trade before this potential reversal occurs.

Price Action based Take Profit

Earlier in this book, I talked about a Price Action setup where Support can become Resistance or vice versa. These setups often point to important levels where the price might change direction.

Now, let me explain how I use this setup to exit my trades using an example.

Picture this: You're in a Long trade which is in an open profit. But suddenly, you notice that the price is getting very close to a zone where there was a Price Action Support that has turned into Resistance. You don't want to take the risk of the price turning around at this Resistance level and wiping out your trade, right? So, you exit the trade a couple of pips (just to be sure) before the Resistance.

Example #1: Price Action based Take Profit

In the picture below, you can see the price reacting to the 1st VWAP Deviation, represented by the grey line. By the way, this setup is known as the VWAP Trend Setup.

A good spot to consider taking your profit is at a point where previous Support has now become Resistance. This Resistance level can act as a barrier. It might stop the Long trade from continuing upward and could cause the price to reverse downward.

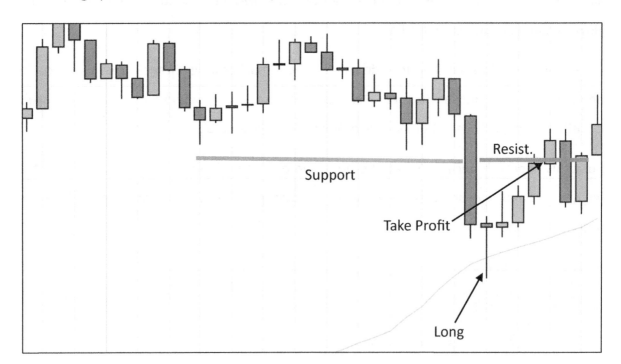

Example #2: Price Action based Take Profit

The picture below shows the price reacting to the 1st VWAP deviation from below (this is the VWAP Rotation setup). A good place to exit the trade is at the Support level that formed as a result of an old Price Action Resistance being breached.

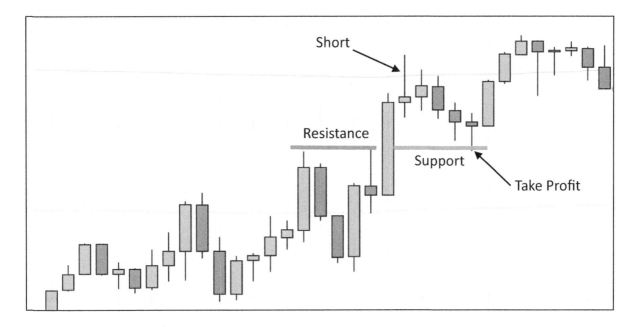

VWAP based Take Profit

The same concept applies to VWAP-based Take Profit. It's all about quitting your trade before it hits a barrier. In this case, that barrier is the VWAP-based Support or Resistance.

Let's say you're in a Short trade, and it's going well. Now, you're thinking about where to close the trade and lock in your profit. The ideal spot is before the price gets to the VWAP Support. It doesn't matter which specific VWAP strategy you use to identify that Support – it could be based on swing points, volume, weekly VWAP, and so on. But when you spot a VWAP support, it's a smart move to exit the trade a bit early, just a few pips before the price reaches it. Why? Because there's a risk that the price will react to this support, reverse, and potentially ruin your trade.

Example #1: VWAP-based Take Profit

The picture below illustrates the VWAP Rotation setup with the price hitting the 1st VWAP deviation from below and reacting to it. In this scenario, the best place to take your profit is at the VWAP line (yellow line).

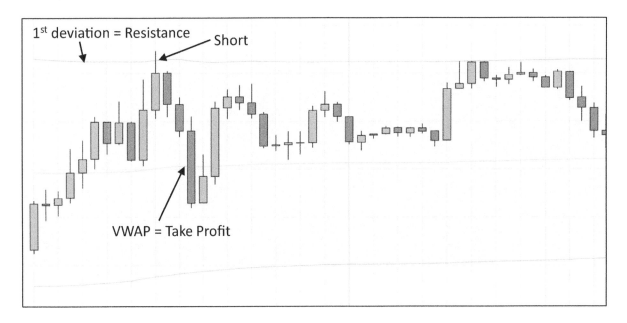

Example #2: VWAP-based Take Profit

The picture below displays the VWAP anchored at a significant swing low. After some time, there is a pullback to this VWAP, providing a nice Long trade entry.

The logical trade exit is determined by the VWAP anchored at a crucial zone - the beginning of a strong trend. In this case, it was best to close the trade as soon as it reached this significant VWAP-based Resistance.

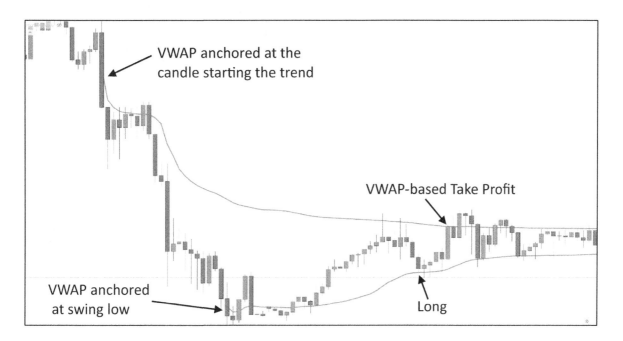

Example #3: VWAP-based Take Profit

In this case, the short trade entry is based on VWAP anchored at an important swing high.

A good exit point for the trade is where the price encounters another VWAP anchored at a significant swing low, representing strong Support.

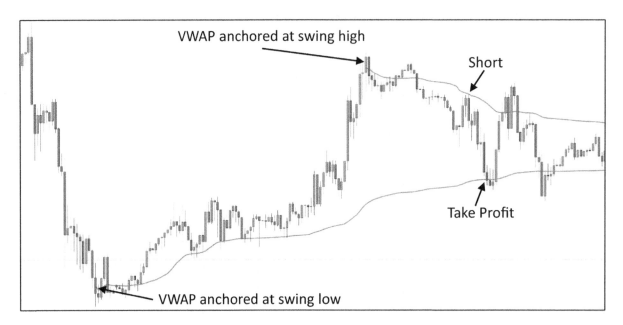

I'd like to mention a quick tip here. If you start drawing all the possible VWAPs and anchored VWAPs on your charts, you'll end up with a lot of potential barriers. This could lead to exiting your trade prematurely because you'll see barriers every few pips, right? So, my advice is not to clutter your charts with too many VWAP levels. Focus on the very strong VWAP levels (signals) when you're looking for potential barriers to exit your trade.

Volume Profile based Take Profit

Once more, with this method, we're searching for a barrier that might obstruct our successful trade, and we exit the trade before the price reaches this barrier. In this scenario, the barrier is represented by a heavy volume zone, which you can identify using Volume Profile.

These heavy volume zones often serve as strong Supports and Resistances. That's why it's a good practice to exit your trade a few pips before the price reaches this barrier.

Example #1: Volume Profile-based Take Profit

The picture below shows the price responding positively to a weekly VWAP (yellow line), resulting in a significant upward movement. The optimal point to exit this trade is when the price approaches a heavy volume zone. This heavy-volume zone acts as a Resistance (barrier), which is why it's advisable to exit the trade a few pips before reaching it.

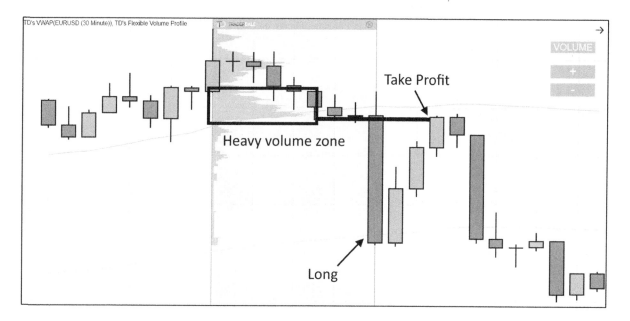

Example #2: Volume Profile-based Take Profit

The image below demonstrates a successful reaction to the Weekly VWAP (yellow line). The best spot to take your profit is just a few pips before the price hits the first heavy volume zone, acting as a barrier (Support).

Although this Support didn't exactly push the price upward, it did slow down the market's momentum, resulting in a sideways movement. In my view, it's wiser to exit the trade at this point rather than spending hours in a sideways price range with no clear direction.

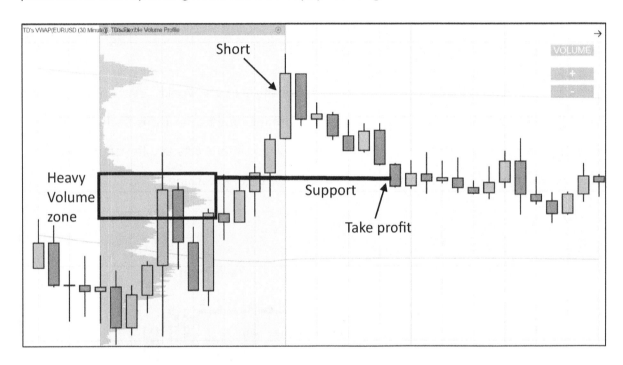

ATR based Take Profit

If, for some reason, you prefer a fixed Take Profit rather than the methods I previously mentioned, you might find this approach suitable. It relies on determining your Take Profit using the average daily volatility of the instrument you are trading.

Let's begin with an example. Suppose EUR/USD exhibits an average daily volatility of 100 pips. As an intraday trader, you would aim to use 10-20% of the average daily volatility as your Take Profit. In this case, your Take Profit would range from 10-20 pips.

Here's how to do it:

Calculating the average daily volatility is a breeze using the ATR (Average True Range) indicator, which is readily available for free in most trading platforms.

Set the ATR for an extended period, like 200. Load approximately 300-500 days' worth of data on your charts in the daily timeframe, and note the average ATR value for this period. This value represents the average daily volatility.

To express this value in pips, multiply the ATR number by 10,000.

For intraday trades, I recommend setting your Take Profit at around 10-20% of the average daily ATR.

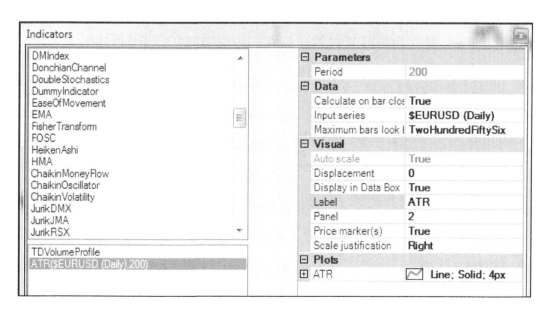

In the example below, there are 500 daily candles for EUR/USD, and the ATR indicator is set to a 200-period timeframe. The ATR value is approximately 0.0085. To find the average daily volatility for EUR/USD in pips, multiply this number by 10,000, resulting in 85 pips. With this example, your intraday Take Profit values should fall within the 8.5 to 17 pip range.

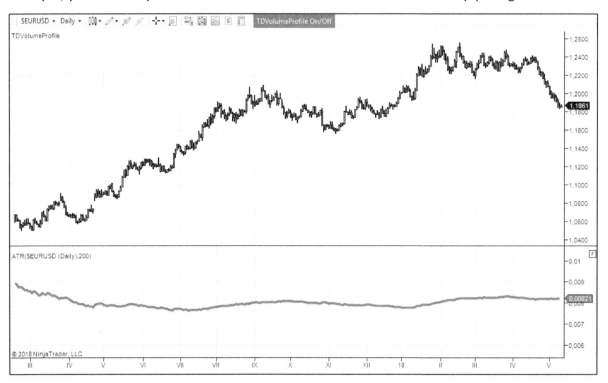

Stop Loss placement

The key rule to remember when setting your Stop Loss is to always position it BEHIND a barrier, which is represented by a Support or Resistance zone. This barrier can be identified through Price Action, VWAP, or Volume Profile analysis.

The reason for putting your Stop Loss behind a barrier is to keep your trade safe. A barrier is a zone that the price should not cross. If the price goes past it, it could mean the trend is changing. Think of the barrier as a safety net for your trade. If it gets crossed, it's a good idea to exit your trade because once it's crossed, we don't know where the price might go next.

Price Action based Stop Loss placement

When you set your Stop Loss using Price Action, a logical choice is to place it at a swing point or a significant high/low. This makes sense because those points were crucial in the past, and the price changed direction there. The assumption is that these levels will continue to be important in the future, and ideally, the price shouldn't reach them if the trend is to continue.

Example #1: Price Action Stop Loss placement

The picture below shows a VWAP Rotation setup and a successful reaction to the 1st VWAP deviation. Stop Loss for this trade should be placed above the nearest swing point.

Example #2: Price Action Stop Loss placement

The picture below shows multiple viable short trades – all based on the VWAP Trend setup. In each case, Stop Loss should go at the previous high.

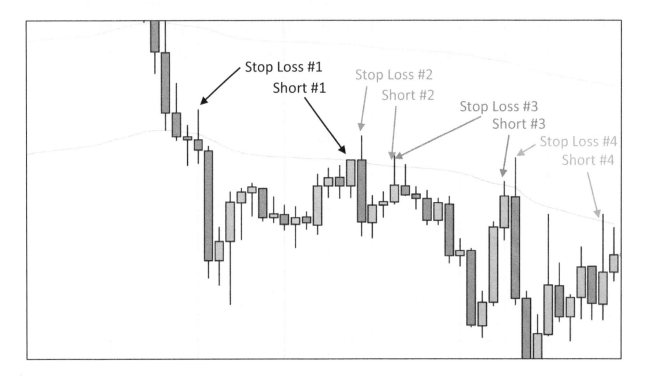

VWAP based Stop Loss placement

VWAP and its Deviations act like strong Support or Resistance zones, which can be thought of as barriers. It's a wise approach to place your Stop Loss behind one of these barriers.

Example #1: VWAP Stop Loss placement

The image below displays a good opportunity for a Long trade. This is based on a pullback to a VWAP that's anchored at an important swing low.

Even though this VWAP has been tested before, it still acts as a reliable support. As the price continues to rise, the VWAP also rises and serves as a solid barrier. You can place your Stop Loss behind it and adjust it higher as the price goes up.

As you can observe, the price eventually moves significantly above the VWAP. In such a case, I recommend searching for other Support levels to move your Stop Loss to because the VWAP is now too far away, and having the Stop Loss behind it would be too distant.

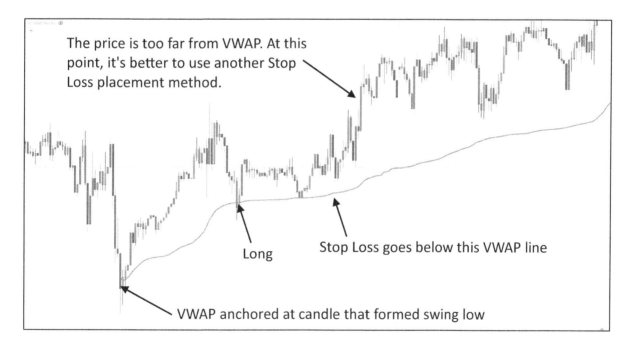

Example #2: VWAP Stop Loss placement

The picture below shows two lines: a blue line - VWAP, anchored at an important swing low, and a yellow line - Weekly VWAP. The yellow line is automatically calculated from the beginning of the week, and there are also two grey lines representing its deviations.

To enter a trade, I look for a pullback to the VWAP anchored at the swing point. At this point I recommend placing Stop Loss below the blue VWAP line.

However, as the price keeps going up, the Stop Loss initially placed below the VWAP (blue line) becomes too far away. In this situation, it's a good idea to find another level to use as a Stop Loss.

I recommend using the first VWAP and its deviations at this point. Initially, you can place the Stop Loss below the lower deviation. When the price continues to rise, you can then move it up below the yellow Weekly VWAP line. As the price goes even higher, you can further adjust the Stop Loss below the upper deviation. Eventually, the Stop Loss at this level is hit, marking a successful trade exit.

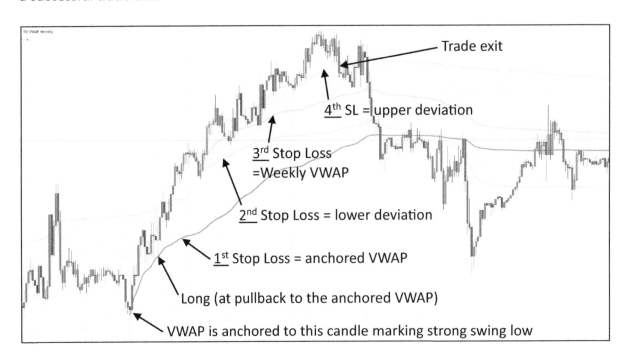

Example #2: VWAP Stop Loss placement

The picture below shows a short trade example using the VWAP Trend setup.

Here, the price is trending downwards, going below a lower VWAP deviation (represented by a grey line). To enter a short trade, we wait for the price to pull back and touch this lower deviation from below.

Once this happens, a strong downtrend begins. At the start of this downtrend, I anchor the blue VWAP as a reference point for my Stop Loss. If the price crosses this level, I no longer want to stay in the short trade I entered earlier. This breach would signal that the selling pressure has subsided, and there's no reason to continue with the trade.

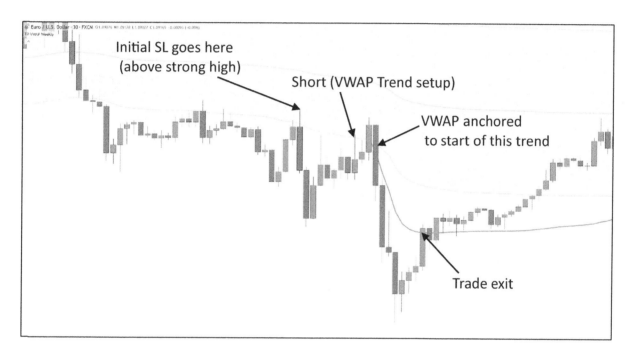

Volume Profile based Stop Loss placement

As mentioned earlier, heavy volume zones are powerful barriers. It's logical to place your Stop Loss behind these barriers. If the barrier gets breached, it's usually a sign that the trade might not go as expected, and it's best to exit.

Example #1: Volume Profile Stop Loss placement

The image below displays a Long trade based on the VWAP Trend setup. The price is in an uptrend, and then it makes a pullback to the upper deviation of the Weekly VWAP. This is where we decide to enter the trade.

The volume-based Stop Loss is placed behind a heavy volume zone which formed within the uptrend. If this barrier is breached, it signifies that sellers have taken control, and there's no good reason to stay in a Long trade anymore.

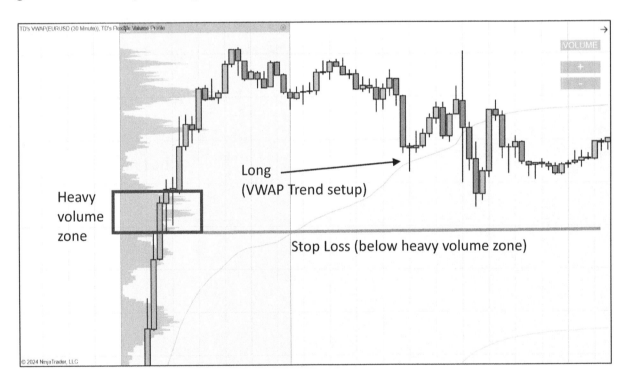

Example #2: Volume Profile Stop Loss placement

The picture below shows a viable short trade starting at the Weekly VWAP.

A suitable location for the Stop Loss is behind a heavy volume zone that formed during the downtrend.

A good place to take profit is at the lower VWAP deviation because it might act as Support and cause the price to move upward.

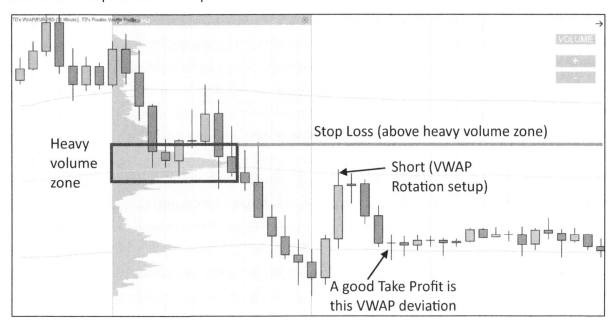

Stop Loss placement – combined barriers

You should aim to place your Stop Loss behind a very strong barrier. This barrier could be a combination of elements like a heavy volume zone and a swing point or a heavy volume zone and VWAP. The stronger the barrier, the better.

However, don't set your Stop Loss too far away because if you're trailing your trade in a trend and it reverses, you don't want to lose all your profits. So, if there isn't a super strong barrier nearby, a weaker one that's closer will suffice.

Here are some examples of these combined barriers:

Example #1: Stop Loss placement – combined barriers

The image below shows a VWAP Trend setup. In this scenario, the price is moving below the Weekly VWAP deviation, then it pulls back to it, creating a nice opportunity for a short trade.

A suitable location for a Stop Loss is behind a heavy volume zone, and also behind a small swing point, which is positioned just after this area with heavy volumes.

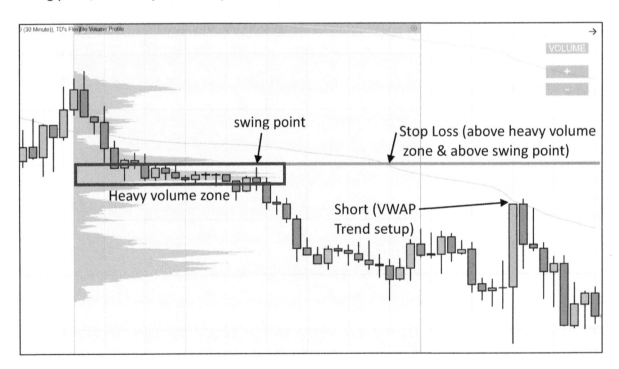

Example #2: Stop Loss placement – combined barriers

The image below displays a VWAP Rotation setup. Here, the price is moving inside a sideways corridor formed by the upper and lower deviations of the Weekly VWAP. A signal to enter a short trade occurs when the price touches the upper deviation from below.

A smart spot to set a Stop Loss is behind a heavy volume zone. This zone acts as a barrier. Also, it is positioned above a swing point that the price should not cross if it is to continue moving downward.

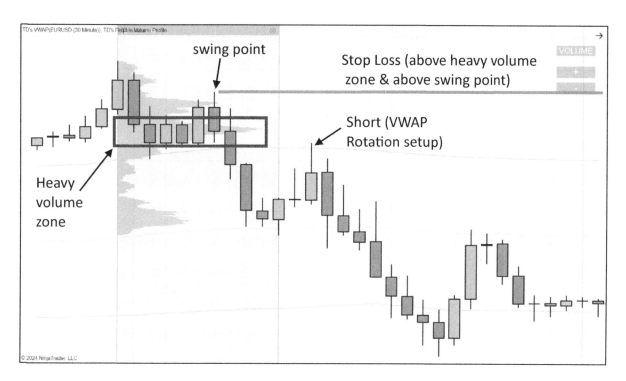

ATR based Stop Loss

An alternative approach to Stop Loss placement is to use a fixed Stop Loss based on the ATR method, which I previously discussed when explaining Take Profit placement. For intraday trades, a reasonable Stop Loss size is typically around 10-20% of the average daily volatility of the instrument you're trading.

You can also apply this approach when there isn't any other viable level (based on Price Action, VWAP, or Volume Profile) to position your Stop Loss.

Trailing your trade

If you managed to jump into a strong trend, for example at a pullback, you might want to consider trailing your trade. Riding a strong trend can lead to a nice profit.

To trail your trade, continuously adjust your Stop Loss (moving it higher in an uptrend) as the trend develops, like in this example:

Example #1: Trailing your trade

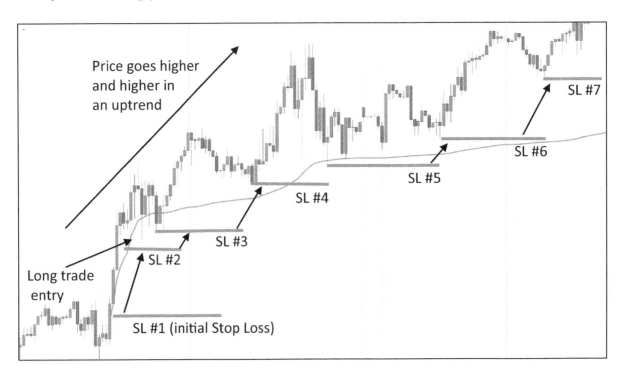

However, when adjusting your Stop Loss during a trend, remember to follow the rules I discussed earlier. This means always placing your Stop Loss behind a strong Price Action, VWAP, or Volume Profile barrier.

Example #2: Trailing your trade

The example below illustrates the VWAP Trend setup, where the price reacts to the Weekly VWAP deviation by touching it from below.

Initially, place your Stop Loss behind a barrier of heavy volumes, and also above an important swing point.

As the price moves lower, the next sensible step is to adjust your Stop Loss above the next swing point, the one that forms when the price reacts to the VWAP deviation. Additionally, there is another heavy volume zone just below this swing point.

The next adjustment for your Stop Loss should be behind the following zone with heavy volumes.

As the price continues to drop, the next move to safeguard your open profit even more is to place your Stop Loss behind the next heavy volume zone that forms as the price keeps dropping.

This will be your final Stop Loss, as the price turns and touches it, which results in ending the trade.

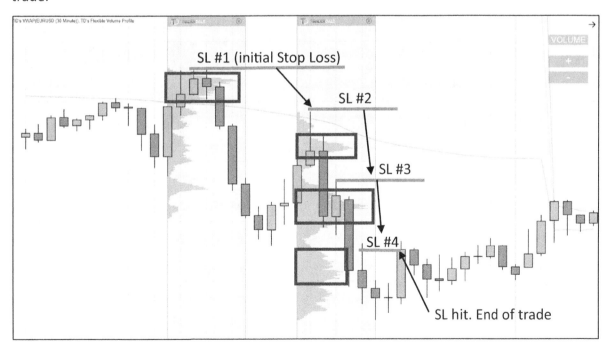

Example #3: Trailing your trade

In the example below, you can see a Long trade based on the VWAP Trend setup. The price moves above the upper deviation of the Weekly VWAP and then retraces to it. This is the signal to enter a Long trade.

In this example, we adjust the Stop Loss as the trend continues upwards. Here is a list of the places to move the Stop Loss to, along with a brief explanation of why to move it to each specific location:

- Initial Stop Loss (SL #1): This Stop Loss is placed behind a heavy volume zone.
- SL #2: The Stop Loss is positioned behind a heavy volume barrier and below a swing point.
- SL #3: The Stop Loss is set behind a heavy volume barrier and below a swing point.
- SL #4: The Stop Loss is positioned behind a heavy volume barrier.
- SL #5: The Stop Loss is located behind a heavy volume barrier. This serves as the final Stop Loss.

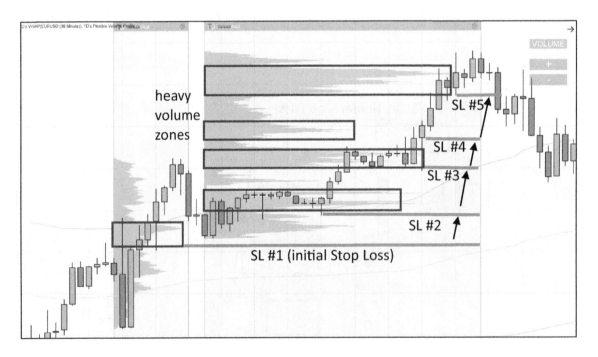

Avoid placing your Stop Loss too far away. If you're trailing your trade within a trend and the trend suddenly reverses, having a very distant Stop Loss could lead to losing all your earned profit. So, ideally, position your Stop Loss behind a strong barrier.

But if there's no exceptionally strong barrier nearby, a weaker one closer to your current position should suffice.

Keep in mind that when trailing a trade within a trend, the key is to keep your position safe by continuously adjusting your Stop Loss as the trend unfolds.

Start simple

As you can see from what I've shown you, there are many ways to handle your trades, from deciding when to enter a trade to setting your profit target and stop loss. I understand it might feel a bit overwhelming. Think of it as a list of options I can share based on my experience. You don't have to use them all right away. Start by choosing one or two methods for entering and exiting trades. Get really good at them until they feel natural to you. Then, if you want, you can explore more of the possibilities I mentioned.

If I were to suggest a starting point, it would be this:

Trade Entry confirmation: Use the "Entering a trade after a successful reaction" approach. This means entering a trade when you see the market reacting to Support/Resistance levels (like when a candle closes above Support or below Resistance).

Stop Loss placement: The entry method I mentioned earlier always provides a good swing point at the place where the price reacted. This is the right place for your Stop Loss.

Take Profit Placement: Aim for a Risk Reward Ratio (RRR) of 1. If your Stop Loss is, for example, 15 pips, set your Take Profit at 15 pips as well. It's easy!

Here's an example of how a trade like this could look like:

Entry Level: This short trade begins with a pullback to VWAP, which is anchored at the candle that marked the start of a significant downtrend.

Confirmation for Entry: To confirm the trade entry, look for a bullish candle closing below VWAP.

Stop Loss: Set at the reaction point.

Take Profit: Calculate it based on the Stop Loss to maintain a Risk Reward Ratio (RRR) of 1.

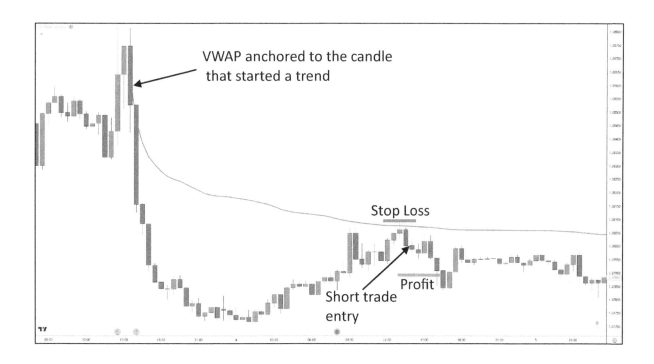

VWAP anchored to the candle
that started a trend

Stop Loss

Short trade
entry

Profit

Another example:

<u>Entry Level:</u> This short trade begins with a pullback to VWAP, which is anchored at a significant swing high.

<u>Confirmation for Entry:</u> To confirm the trade entry, look for a bullish candle closing below VWAP.

<u>Stop Loss:</u> Set at the reaction point.

<u>Take Profit:</u> Calculate it based on the Stop Loss to maintain a Risk Reward Ratio (RRR) of 1.

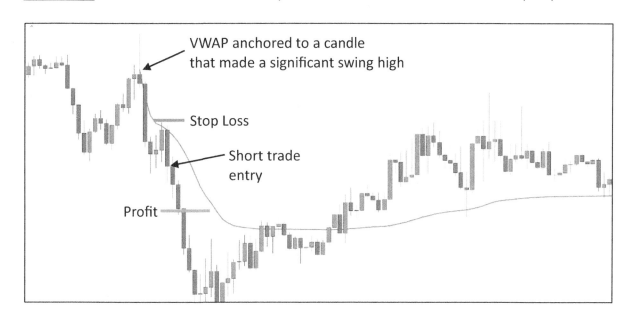

VWAP anchored to a candle
that made a significant swing high

Stop Loss

Short trade
entry

Profit

One last example:

In the picture below, there are three viable trades. All of them start with a pullback to VWAP, which is attached to a candle that created an important swing low.

The first and third trades are fast, in-and-out trades, while the second trade is a larger one that takes more time to develop.

The confirmation for trade entry, placement of Stop Loss, and setting Take Profit are the same as in the two earlier examples.

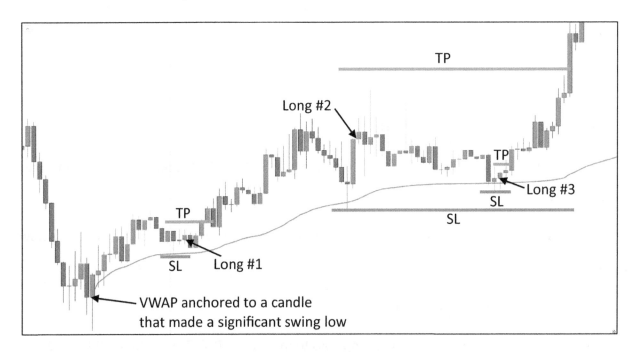

Money management

Managing your money is a crucial part of any trading plan. Even if your trading strategy is great, you might lose money if you don't handle your money wisely.

Risk per trade

One of the most important things in managing your money while trading is how much you're willing to risk on each trade. Here's a simple way to figure it out:

1. Start by backtesting your trading strategy. This will show you how your strategy performed over time. The most crucial thing you'll learn from this is the biggest loss your strategy had in the past, known as the "drawdown." Keep in mind that real trading conditions can be a bit worse than what you see in the backtest, maybe around 20% worse.

2. Let's say your strategy's worst drawdown was 6 consecutive losses. With the 20% factor included, you'd estimate it as 6 x 1.2 = 7.2 losses. So, in the worst-case scenario, you can expect 7 losing trades in a row.

3. Now, think about how much of your trading account balance you're comfortable losing without getting too worried. This comfort level varies for each person. For example, you might be okay with a 25% loss, but it could be different for someone else. An ambitious young trader might be fine with a 50% drawdown, while a more experienced trader with a larger account could be upset about a 10% loss.

4. Let's say you're mentally prepared for a 25% drawdown. In this case, those 7 losing trades should represent the 25% loss. To calculate how much to risk on each trade, divide the 25% by the number of trades, which is 7. This gives you the percentage of your trading capital to risk per trade, which is 25% / 7 = 3.6%.

So, based on this simple calculation, you should risk 3.6% of your trading capital on each trade.

Position sizing

It's really important to use the same amount of money for all your trades. For instance, if you decide to risk 2% of your account balance on each trade, make sure you always follow this rule. The specific number of pips for your Stop Loss or Take Profit can vary from trade to trade, but the percentage you risk should stay consistent.

Some traders like to change the amount they risk based on how confident they feel about a trade. If they're really sure about a trade, they might risk more, and if they're unsure, they might risk less. However, I'm not a fan of this approach for two reasons. First, feelings are hard to measure, so it's not a reliable method. Second, in my experience, even trades that don't look perfect can be just as successful as the ones that seem flawless. Actually, I've seen many seemingly perfect trades go wrong. So, I prefer to stick to a solid plan and use the same position size for all my trades.

Trade manager (software)

You might agree that calculating how much to trade for each trade can be a hassle. That's why I made a tool called the Trade Manager. It does this math for me automatically. But that's not all it does. Let me quickly tell you about its useful features.

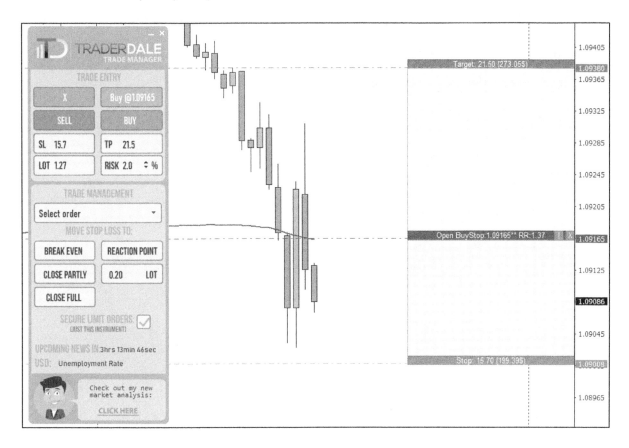

1. Calculating Position Size: You can set how much you're willing to risk on each trade as a percentage, and my tool figures out the lot size for you. This makes placing orders quick and keeps your risk consistent.

2. Adjust Take Profit & Stop Loss: Easily change your Take Profit and Stop Loss levels with a single click. You can see in real-time how it affects your Risk & Reward.

3. Simplified Limit Orders: Placing Limit Orders is made simple with just two clicks. You can even set alerts for when the price gets close.

4. Protecting Your Trade: You can move your Stop Loss to the break-even point or where the price first reacted with just one click to secure your position.

5. Partial Position Closure: Close a part of your trade with a single click. This is useful when you need to act quickly.

6. Secure Limit Orders: This unique feature monitors macroeconomic news and temporarily removes your Limit Orders a few minutes before major news releases to protect your positions from sudden price spikes. After the news, it automatically puts your Limit Orders back in place!

And the best part? It's all FREE! There are no limitations, and you get a lifetime license with no strings attached. Just download it and use it! I am confident you'll love it, and if you do, please share it with your friends. They can use it for free too!

Here's the link to get it: https://mt4trademanager.com

What to do next

In this book, I have done my best to explain how to trade effectively using VWAP and AVWAP, and I believe I have provided all the essential information that this format allows. If you enjoyed it and would like to bring your VWAP trading to the next level, I recommend your next best step be the special **VWAP Pack** I have made for you. The pack includes:

1. **VWAP Video Course:** A comprehensive 9-hour video course spread over 31 in-depth videos, in which I detail my VWAP & AVWAP trading strategy.

2. **VWAP & Anchored VWAP Software:** A set of custom-made VWAP and Anchored VWAP indicators for NinjaTrader 8, TradingView, Metatrader 4, and Metatrader 5 trading platforms, including a lifetime and multiple-computer license.

3. **Volume Profile Software:** A suite of custom-made Volume Profile indicators for NinjaTrader 8, TradingView, and Metatrader 4 trading platforms.

BONUS: As a special bonus, our specially trained tech support will complete the setup for you! They will configure the platform, connect it to data, install all the indicators, and give you a guided tour!

Get the VWAP Pack here:

https://www.trader-dale.com/vwap-training-course-and-indicators/

VWAP PACK

VWAP Video Course

- 31 In-depth videos with 9+ hours of training
- The most profitable VWAP setups I use each day
- How to use VWAP together with Volume Profile
- How to use trade in all market conditions
- How to trail your trades with VWAP and get the most of them

VWAP & Anchored VWAP Software

- Multiple Computers / Lifetime Access
- Supported platforms:
  - NinjaTrader 8
  - TradingView
  - MetaTrader 4 & 5

Volume Profile Software

- Ideal tool to use together with VWAP
- Multiple Computers / Lifetime Access
- Supported platforms:
  - NinjaTrader 8
  - TradingView
  - MetaTrader 4 & 5

The VWAP Pack is available at: www.trader-dale.com

Just a few testimonials on the course

Daniel Dellinger (US)

Prior to taking Dales Volume Profile and Order flow courses and uses his custom tools I was doing terrible. I wasn't ready, didn't really know how volume, order flow related. I was a previous indicator trader (ema, rsi, macd) and never able to reach profitability.

I can say now, I am a profitable trader who no longer uses any indicator except the VWAP.

I also like that the courses didn't take months to complete. Dale gets to the point in his message without labouring on with details that are not needed.

I highly recommend Trader Dales education and tools. I am very satisfied.

Daniele (IT):

I have been a member of the Trader Dale community for some time now, and I must say that the quality of education, tools, and support provided is outstanding. The educational resources offered by Trader Dale have greatly improved my trading skills and knowledge. The courses are well-structured, comprehensive, and easy to follow, making it accessible even for beginners like myself.

Corey Cepeda (US)

The video content is super easy to digest and understand. Any combination of material will raise your trading IQ. I have seen a great uptick in winning trades with Dale's system. I expect great things as I understand more.

Chucks Ihearahu (GB)

I find your course excellent and of great value for the money compared to other online courses I have looked into. Dale keeps it simple and updates you every day with levels that work.

Martin Veljanoski (MK)

Wonderful experience. Everything that one trader should need to know before starting trading on one place from literature to implementing real strategies with some sophisticated, real and advances tools. It's just everything clicks after the course. The support team was unimaginable fast and responsive on every question that I have on my mind. All in one, just worth the time to spend if anyone looking for good and effective educational background before starting trading.

Mark Richberg (US)

WOW!! What a great experience I have had with Dale, this software and his customer support over the years. I purchased this software about 2 years ago after I read his free ebook on Volume-based trading and Big institutions. What a great read.

I ended up purchasing ALL of his products (Volume, Order Flow Elite pack, Stock pack - all of them) and I have not been disappointed!

Dale explains complex topics very clearly in his free articles and training videos. Over time (I have watched all of his videos at least twice) I understand more and more and this has greatly advanced my trading skills the last 2 years.

But what sets Dale's business apart is his customer service. He always answers emails, responds to service requests in his Discord chat (a group of his customers from around the world!) quickly and effectively.

On the customer service note, his tech guy Jason just solved a MAJOR issue for me concerning my Cumulative Delta indicator. That issue has been troubling me for YEARS and I could not figure it out. There was a compatibility issue with other Indicators. I scheduled an appointment through Dale's easy to use appointment system and JASON came to my rescue!

I cannot over emphasize Jason's patience, availability and technical expertise in both Dale's software and NinjaTrader. His absolute refusal to quit until the problem was fixed was impressive and I am very grateful!

I would not hesitate to give both Dale's products and Jason's Technical support skills, knowledge and courtesy my highest recommendation!

Randy Latsch (US)

Dale puts out new levels daily so you can trade almost immediately while learning this strategy. If you stay with his system long enough you can accurately trade most any market. Many tools and indicators available with easy-to-understand videos. This course is very valuable even if you have your own strategy, as you can use it for confluence or divergence. (I do) I have never had an unanswered email. Communication is awesome. Thanks Dale

Frank Liu (US)

The contents of Trader Dale's courses are very clear-cut and logical. I feel they are suitable for all levels of experiences in trading. On top, the online Support is very resourceful when needed. I personally think Dale took quite a lot of time/efforts putting them together They are really gold-stars, IMO.

Naomi (AU)

Trader Dale has helped me become a more confident and better trader, as a result of his extensive educational offerings (courses, daily trading videos, and e-books). He does not stop teaching - if something significant occurs in a particular market, he'll make a video the same day to share with his members. Specifically, Dale taught me how to understand Price Action and the rationales for price movement. Dale has responded quickly to my emails for 3 years. I've purchased most of his courses and software, which I use to trade the ES (except cumulative delta, which I found to be inaccurate on ES). Dale truly cares about retail traders, because he knows the pitfalls of trading.

Thank you!

At this place, I would like to thank you for reading my book. I hope you liked it, and that you found it useful. I hope it helps you in achieving your financial goals and dreams no matter how big they are!

Happy trading!

-Dale

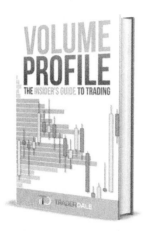

VOLUME PROFILE
The Insider's Guide To Trading

Volume Profile is a fantastic tool to track the activity of the big institutional traders and allows you to trade alongside them rather than against them.

The book details my favorite Volume Profile setups along with practical guides on position and money management, macro news trading, trading psychology, and much more!

ORDER FLOW
Trading Setups

Order Flow is the ultimate tool for intraday trading. It lets you see every executed trading order and monitors the actions of major trading institutions.

In addition to my favorite Order Flow setups, the book will also instruct you on how to determine whether buyers or sellers are dominating the market, how to identify significant institutional orders, how to precisely time your trade entries and exits, and more.

STOCK INVESTING
with Volume Profile

Did you know that 5% inflation will devour 40% of your savings in 10 years? But it won't happen if you take action!

The goal of this book is to teach you how to invest your money smartly, how to build and manage your portfolio, and how to do all this with as little effort as possible.

Made in the USA
Las Vegas, NV
21 March 2025

19940178R00070